Back in Control

A Woman's Journey of Managing Unexpected Changes

Jyothika Shetty

Back in Control
Copyright © 2020 Jyothika Shetty
First published in 2020

ISBN
Print: 978-1-922456-10-6
E-book: 978-1-922456-11-3

All rights reserved. No part of this book may be reproduced, stored in a retrieval system, or transmitted by any means (electronic, mechanical, photocopying, recording, or otherwise) without written permission from the author.

Because of the dynamic nature of the Internet, any web addresses or links contained in this book may have changed since publication and may no longer be valid. The information in this book is based on the author's experiences and opinions. The views expressed in this book are solely those of the author and do not necessarily reflect the views of the publisher; the publisher hereby disclaims any responsibility for them.

The author of this book does not dispense any form of medical, legal, financial, or technical advice either directly or indirectly. The intent of the author is solely to provide information of a general nature to help you in your quest for personal development and growth. In the event you use any of the information in this book, the author and the publisher assume no responsibility for your actions. If any form of expert assistance is required, the services of a competent professional should be sought.

Publishing information
Publishing, design, and production facilitated by Passionpreneur Publishing,
A division of Passionpreneur Organization Pty Ltd, ABN: 48640637529

www.PassionpreneurPublishing.com
Melbourne, VIC | Australia

TESTIMONIALS

A perfect book at the right time. A must-read that gets you prepared to manage the unexpected change in unprecedented times. Jyothika's story is so compelling that it lets you pause and think so you can handle things differently, which bring new experiences that matter, as we should not go back to old routes because that is easy. We should take the journey to let ourselves get inspired and energized by reading this book. Enjoy and Bon Voyage.

Sophie Ho, MBA
Investor Relations Manager
Founder of KoBeautique
Holland, The Netherlands

Many may want to write a book but few can go through with it. I am not surprised that an amazing woman, Jyothika, has completed her book. With her tenacity, commitment, and intelligence, this dynamic and forward-looking young woman had to inspire other women to bring out their talents and learn to believe in themselves. Change is the only constant, and adapting to change is how we succeed in life. This is a must-read for all women.

Hearty congratulations, Jyothika. Keep rising. Keep shining.

Dunstanette L. Macauley
Past Region 11 Advisor, Toastmasters International
CEO—ICBM Events Sarl

Back in Control *helps you to bounce back in life... Whatever goes up, has to come down and vice versa, but taking control of your life ensures your victory over hurdles. Winners never quit, and even if they have to take a break, they come back with more energy and achieve their goals.* Back in control *will definitely inspire you to stand up again one more time, take control of your life, and fulfill your dreams.*

I wish Jyothika all the very best for her first release.

Sundeep Kochar
TEDx Speaker, Coach and Celebrity Astrologer
Limca Book of World Record Holder
Mumbai, India

Jyothika is a dynamic global leader and dedicated woman of power. Her organizational leadership and exceptional communication mastery make her one of the most prominent professionals in her field. I can attest to Jyothika's expertise in managing change. As one of the primary facilitators of my first World Public Speaking Tour, Jyothika created clear and punctilious strategies for marketing and public relations. She executed those strategies reliably and effectively. In addition, I was astonished by her propensity to perfectly balance work life and family time. I encourage readers to dive into this book. Become fully immersed in the ocean of knowledge Jyothika is gifting.

Ramona J. Smith
Author and Professional Speaker
World Champion of Public Speaking (2018,
Toastmasters International)
Cleveland, Ohio

Jyothika has been a great example for "Change." She embraced the constant changes in her life and managed them so well. As life would have it, she always wanted to do more. With her valuable life experience, she is able to connect to her audience very well. Her firsthand experiences and having witnessed changes happening to people in her inner circle makes it just apt for her to be "An Author."

Veena D'Silva
Head-Talent Acquisition
Mumbai, India

It's not every day that you meet someone who is ready to reinvent themselves while they are settled in life. Jyothika is one individual I have come across who is hungry to grow relentlessly and help those around her to grow. The passion she puts into every project she undertakes, be it her MBA in her 40s, or her Toastmaster leadership role, or growing as an entrepreneur, author, and motivational speaker—there are no ceilings to her goals. She constantly aspires for more, and her life becomes a testament to all of us on how we should never give up and always strive to constantly push the envelope to be the very best version of ourselves.

Samir Geepee
Life Coach, Author
Dubai, UAE

Table of Contents

Foreword		ix
Author Biography		xiii
Acknowledgments		xv
Introduction		xix
I am a Woman . . . A tribute to all women out there!		xxix
Chapter 1	Emotional Intelligence and the Leader in You	1
Chapter 2	The Yolk in the Egg	9
Chapter 3	Emotional Intelligence in Decision-Making	21
Chapter 4	The Fork in the Road	27
Chapter 5	Emotional Intelligence and Attitude	43
Chapter 6	Your Attitude Determines Your Altitude	49
Chapter 7	Emotional Intelligence in Managing Stress	63
Chapter 8	The Illusion Called Success	71
Chapter 9	Emotional Intelligence and Empathy	85
Chapter 10	The Divine Storm	91
Chapter 11	Managing Unexpected Change	103
Chapter 12	The Road to Self-Discovery	109
Conclusion		125
References		135

Foreword

IT IS OFTEN said that champions are not those who never fall down. Champions are those who get back up to fight again. I believe that's the same in the journey of life. While everyone has good days and bad days, not everyone has what it takes to get back up after a massive setback.

This timely book by Jyothika is a wake-up call for women to know that no matter what happened to you, it is not over yet—you can get back in control. During your journey of life, whenever your vehicle skids off the road, you can consciously choose to be the driver of your life to get back onto the best path and move ahead. Throughout this book Jyothika weaves the lessons she learned from her life and from renowned experts to provide you with specific action points that you can use to achieve a better outcome in your life.

The beauty of this book lies in the vulnerability of the author to show her struggles, dilemmas, and inner conversations that you would be able to relate to. Such insights into oneself is the key to self-awareness and informed action. Having known

Jyothika over the past three years, and having worked with her during her pursuit of self-discovery, I can attest to the sincerity, authenticity, and eagerness she has to help other women— and the courage to share the personal story of her life.

While this is essentially a book written by a courageous woman to help other women find courage, there is a lesson there for anyone who wants to get back in control without giving up. The principles listed in this book are timeless and effective for those who are willing to take determined action.

When something is lost, not everything is lost. When things don't go your way, it is not all over. You can write a new chapter of your life. When you have to chart a new path, you need a new map; you need to find people who can guide you on that path. As you read this book, Jyothika will come across as the guide you were looking for.

The key to your success is your belief in a better outcome and understanding that life is in the journey, not the destination. This means you are always challenging, stretching, and striving out of your comfort zone. In that process, you will learn more about yourself and grow as a person who is able to do more and be more. As you are striving you need to make important life decisions. As Jyothika says, you will often face a fork in the road in your journey. Each path will provide you with different challenges, experiences, and potential outcomes.

As you go through the chapters of this book with Jyothika, imagine that you are retracing your own journey from childhood, realizing who you truly are, who your influencers are,

FOREWORD

and what shaped your current beliefs. However, the reason to look back is not to regret, but to look forward with determined action—not to repeat the same mistakes—but to repeat what works.

In your journey of life, when there is a bump in the road, fork in the road, or when you skid off the road, allow Jyothika to be your guide to get back on your feet and get back in control.

I wish you well as you accelerate your life's journey in the direction of your dreams.

Manoj Vasudevan
Next Level Leadership Readiness Expert
World Champion of Public Speaking
CEO Thought Expressions
www.ThoughtExpressions.com

Author Biography

The only source of knowledge is experience

—*Albert Einstein*

JYOTHIKA IS A corporate professional having a cumulative experience of over 20 years in the field of risk and financial management, entrepreneurship, and public speaking. Her experience is attributed to her career in the field of corporate banking and family-owned construction business in Dubai. Having spent the majority of her life in Dubai-UAE, she is the second generation to be living there.

Being a woman in family-owned business, she has gained an insight into the opportunities and challenges that women in business face. She is also well experienced in the strategies that help family businesses succeed in their mission.

Jyothika is a certified compliance practitioner, accredited by the International Compliance Association, UK, and also holds an MBA degree from Manchester Business School, UK. A passionate public speaker and writer, Jyothika has mentored aspiring leaders and newbies in the field of leadership and public speaking.

With her rich experience in family business, her focus has been, since then, on several leadership roles, coaching people to conquer their fear of public speaking, and overcoming their limiting self-belief. She has also guided and motivated them to take up leadership roles and lead from the front.

Her passion is to motivate people to come forward, take charge, and be on the top of their game. She is passionate about topics such as leadership, mentoring, teamwork, and emotional intelligence and believes that success is the result of engaging teams effectively. Her hobbies include writing poems and short articles inspired by the daily experiences of life. Her mantra of life is "Be a lifelong learner" as this is a key to be in tune with reality.

She is a great listener and has an awesome way of connecting with people and sharing her stories through lessons learned. You may reach out to Jyothika Shetty at jyothika@jyothikashetty.com, LinkedIn: Jyothika75 or through her website www.jyothikashetty.com.

Acknowledgments

From Thinker to an Author

As kids, creating a life was never a priority because life was all about experiencing and living it. But as you grow up, experiences become scarce in the wake of conditions that we have to abide by; for example, life will be happy if you complete that degree, get that job, or achieve social status. One begins to believe that happiness is found only when you achieve something, and this puts us on an endless pursuit of running behind goals. As you grow, words such as "create" and "found" are used in the same narrative as one starts believing that happiness is *found* when we *create* what we want. Creating a life, creating a career, creating a business are some of the standards that we set for ourselves in order to be happy.

During the growth phase, you are not really concerned about losing what you have earned because you are totally focused on making things happen. When you hit the roadblock, you stand up again in pursuit of your defined happiness and goals. Commitment and perseverance becomes a part of your personality as all you want is to attain that goal. Any failure faced at this phase of your life does not throw you out of control but instead gives you more reasons to get up and move ahead. This is the journey upward for every human being and it could be a journey of building that great business, getting that dream job, or even having that beautiful family. These possessions make you believe that you are totally in control of your life and can conquer the world.

This book begins with my life experience from childhood and exploring people and incidents that shaped my personality. It takes you through a journey of challenges and triumphs that I faced head-on and saw many moments of success. I was in control as our business did well and kids moved in the right direction. It felt that this life was easy to handle and nothing was beyond my reach. But little did I know that the life I had was not the complete story because the best was yet to come. Life was about to teach me some valuable lessons, and this is where I had to start looking at life in a different perspective. It is something like how the GPS starts recalculating the distance to your destination when you change your path. This is when I came across myriad experiences that truly made my life worth living. In this book, I share my experiences with a view that it could be your guide to handling life in the wake of an unexpected turn of events that could potentially throw life out of control.

The unexpected changes that I faced in my life changed a lot of things for me. Although initially I thought it was all too harsh on me, this has been the most satisfying journey till date. This is because I chose to experience every bit of this experience as a learning and evolve as a better person than sinking in the ocean of doubt. Mine is a journey of trial and errors, and although I am not there yet, I have certainly come a long way with an experience worth sharing.

My pillars of strength during the testing times were my mother, my husband, and my three children without whom I would not have got back in control. A few friends have helped me sail through the rough times just by keeping a check on me and making me believe in the power of words. I am also grateful to my mentors and coaches who, at different stages, were instrumental in identifying my inner strength and guiding me toward growth. A special thank-you to all my protégés who have helped me to help them and because of whom I could realize my passion and direction in life.

The main narrative in this book is my personal journey and how at one point it came spiraling down. Later, it is about how I chose to become emotionally aware by focusing on the lessons and used them as a powerful tool to create a well-balanced life. I have thus shared my life lessons in six main chapters discussing the following key aspects that helped me bring my life back in control.

1. Self-awareness
2. Decision-making
3. Attitude
4. Stress management
5. Empathy
6. Managing unexpected change

Each of these six chapters is linked to six other chapters that discuss the role of emotional intelligence in improving these key aspects.

Understanding my journey better at every stage has helped me to understand my emotions better and balance them at a later stage in my life. I do not claim to be an expert in emotional intelligence, but this is an attempt to narrate my real-life experience and the role of emotional intelligence in my life. The theoretical aspect in this book is drawn from the previous works of experts in this field and the information available on this subject.

While the book has the potential to resonate with anyone who faces unexpected change, the primary objective is to reach out to women over mid-thirties. This is a crucial time period in a life of a woman as she starts facing the highs and lows of life both emotionally and physically. Reaching out to these women is to let them know that you are not alone and you have the power to change your reality.

This entire book is dedicated to my mother, Mrs. Shashikala Shetty, who is the alchemist in my journey.

Introduction

Let me begin by narrating three different stories.

Story 1:
Ria was a software engineer and worked in a multinational firm in India. She always dreamed of having a loving family, a flourishing career, and success that she could be proud of. Indeed, she was lucky and was able to achieve all of that by the time she was 32 years old. There was no looking back, and she was on a roll.

Ria also was an inspiration as she was able to balance her personal and professional life with ease, thanks to her doting husband Vicky and Ria's mother. They were her support system who helped her in the journey of achieving her dream. There was nothing that could shake her confidence or her little world that she was proud of—that is what Ria thought.

Why not? She was a capable, confident, and charismatic woman who could handle any unexpected turbulence that could potentially affect her life. Ria's indomitable spirit and undeterred confidence was her style statement, and it only got stronger each day. Her most cherished dream of owning her house was realized on her 34th birthday, and this ensured security for her entire family. What could possibly go wrong? When Ria was 42 years old, her son joined one of the top colleges in California to pursue his undergrad study in the field of computer engineering. He was standing on the threshold of an exciting career ahead, the door to which was just about to open in a short period of time.

Story 2:
Anita a woman of substance—mother of two lovely girls and a dedicated wife. She was ambitious, and at the age of 40, she built her own business while simultaneously pursuing her career in a semi-government organization. Anita was living in the Gulf with her husband and two daughters whom she adored.

Her elder daughter Andy was in high school when Anita conceived for the second time. The age difference between the two kids and Anita's age to bear another child did not seem conducive. But it did not matter to Anita, and she and her husband Richard were ecstatic to welcome their little baby girl into this world. Pearl, as her little baby girl was named, came in as a wave of fresh energy and life into their marriage of 15 years.

Anita wanted to give the best to her children and always looked for opportunities to increase her income. In this aspect, Richard was not very lucky as his career was just enough to make the ends meet. Anita always strived to get that extra income without complaining. Thus, she set up her own advertising business while being employed full-time. At first it seemed hard, but she had a partner who joined hands with her to help her get this going. Slowly but steadily Anita progressed and also managed to have a dream office in a prestigious location. She signed contracts with prestigious clients who promised more business, which meant a stable source of income. At 45, Anita was on the road to amazing achievement that she planned to look back and proudly talk about.

Story 3:
Bob was a handsome young man who was married to his childhood sweetheart Sheila—the only woman he had known for his entire life. The couple had three adorable kids who were the love of their life. Bob was a tall, handsome man with an athletic persona that could easily make heads turn. He was humble and well-mannered and other than his profession as an insurance consultant, he was a fitness expert who gave personal training to people during his free time.

Bob was Sheila's wind beneath her wings, and she could not think of a life without him. Sheila worked for a local bank, and the couple's dream was to provide the best education for their children. She was a beautiful and smart young woman in her late 30s who was successful in building a world of her own. A handsome husband, adorable kids, and a life they always dreamed of. What more could anyone ask for her?

• • •

Let us look at the commonalities in the three stories that you just read. It is about people who had dreams, worked hard, and created a successful life for themselves. They were willingly enduring the struggles because they had a direction in life and they knew that the current struggles are temporary. These are the steps that each one goes through to achieve their goals—despite the scarcity of resources. There was much clarity in their mind and fierce willingness to achieve their ambition. In fact, they all had created a world that was comfortable, and nothing beyond this reality existed. But the story does not end here.

In the case of Ria, she was very close to her children, and when her son went into college it was quite hard for her to accept this change. Although she was an independent woman, she was in for a surprise. Her son's departure to college created a void that led to consequences like depression and mood swings. She slipped into a deep state of loneliness that even after much effort her husband Vicky could not address. Ria's performance at work was severely affected and even strained her relationship with her husband. At 42, Ria felt a deep void in her life and tried to fill it up with distractions that potentially affected her life. She ended up distancing herself from her family and started leading a life in solace that only she could comprehend. Her life potentially had come to a standstill as Ria had pulled the plugs of her much-celebrated life. Although the reason might seem uncanny, Ria could have been carrying some emotional baggage from the past that could have triggered this situation.

In the case of Anita, she had managed to build a business of her own, and she was thriving with her little family. One day

Anita felt some uneasiness in her lower gut and had gone to the doctor for a checkup only to find out that she was suffering from cervical cancer. Overnight, her family shifted to India for treatment, and Anita was immediately put on chemotherapy. Thankfully, she was only in the first stage of cancer.

For the next few months, her family burnt down all their savings for the treatment and also sold their only house that they had in Bangalore. Her Gulf life vanished in flames, and a long road ahead to recovery was staring at her. Luckily with the help of her ex-employer, she traveled to the United States for a fully sponsored treatment. Anita went with her two kids to the United States and lived there for almost two years.

She recovered fully and returned to India, only to witness her life crumbling down like a pack of cards. Her husband Richard underwent complications due to brain aneurysm and passed away instantly. He was fit as a fiddle, but the development was so fast that nothing could save him. Anita was devastated and lost control of her life as too much was happening too fast. She had lost all her life savings in her treatment and now this blow to the family. Her life after a financial high, spiraled down even before she could make sense of what was happening to her.

Bob and Sheila were happy in their little world. Bob was preparing himself for participating in the bodybuilding show that was to take place in six months. He had transformed in about two months for this long-awaited event that was his dream. One morning when Bob woke up, he could barely speak. The previous day he had attended a party and had some drink that must have affected him, he thought. His distorted vocal cord was not a cause of worry and was overlooked as an infection. When this condition continued for a month, Sheila took him to the doctor for consultation. After several tests, he was diagnosed with throat cancer, and it did not take much time for his little world to collapse. Both Bob and Sheila stayed strong and did what was required, but unfortunately in a year's time, Bob succumbed to his illness. At the age of 41, Sheila was left all alone with her three kids. Without a doubt, her life had spiraled down after it had reached the peak of contentment, happiness, and comfort.

These are not sad stories that I am trying to dull you with, but true stories that accentuate the reality that nothing in life is permanent. Circumstances can nosedive at any time, and this is a fact that one cannot ignore the reality, although one can live in denial for a long time. But not every nosedive is because of your own story. It could be due to situations beyond your control, like the way several countries in the world were forced to be under lockdown due to the danger caused by COVID-19. The virus changed the way people lived their lives and did business. More than ever, people understood that nothing in this world is permanent and one has to be receptive to change. More than the panic, people were struggling to adjust to their new life that was imposed on them.

Can you imagine a pack of cards crashing down after you have invested so much effort to put it together? The experience was something like this. Daily livelihoods, businesses, families, you name it and everything was under the impact of the thick clouds of uncertainty. Likewise, much of what happens in life is not under your control. But time and again we are pushed into a state of panic when unexpected change stares at our doorstep. The anxiety that accompanies the change forces many to make decisions that could be detrimental to their well-being.

But have you ever thought? Change is an opportunity to see the rainbow behind the clouds. It is an opportunity to do what you always wanted to do but was scared of being thrown out of your comfort zone. The age-old adage *"When life throws lemons, learn to make the best lemonade"* is the much-suited mantra during times like these. With the ever-changing economic landscape and social strata, one does not have much choice but to go with the flow. The key here is to avoid embracing change with a "no choice" attitude but be grateful for the opportunities that life has given you by making it a catalyst for your growth. Just like what Paulo Coelho wrote in his book *The Alchemist,* "When you really want something to happen, the whole universe will conspire so that your wish comes true."

After attaining the pinnacle of success, you need just one reason to lose what you have earned—your wealth, social status, or opportunity of growth. That one reason could be a divorce, illness, death of a loved one, job loss, bankruptcy, or even an unexpected natural calamity. Life then comes spiraling down, forcing you to lead a life that you may not be ready for, something like an indefinite lockdown. It is during these times your strength is tested, and that "something" motivates you to discover a completely new world of possibility that otherwise you would have never explored. The unknown zone then activates opportunities to bring back your life in control, provided you want it. This book that you are now reading is about keeping that "something" alive when you know that your life is no more in your control.

Getting back in control does not necessarily mean getting your old life back; as they say—*change is inevitable when you have a greater purpose to serve*. This time when opportunity opens its doors for you, it is to embrace something amazing and an entirely new direction in life. But these doors won't open till the time you want them to open. This book is about how one can handle such an unexpected change in life by creating an entirely different direction from the learnings rather than sulking and creating moments of despair. It is about how you can get your life back in control when it goes spiraling down after you have achieved your level of success—because a fall from greater height hurts even more.

The three stories demonstrate that people seldom prepare themselves internally to face changes. Even if you are aware of the inevitable, your tendency is to live in denial. The road to success is always sweet and memorable, and one is ready to endure any amount of hardship to reach that success. But what people do not realize is that after reaching the pinnacle of success one has to also prepare themselves for change. If you are not prepared to face this change, then when change happens it could be devastating. The problem is not the change itself but your unwillingness to accept the change that makes it hard.

Human beings become complacent and take life for granted until the reality strikes so hard that their entire life goes spiraling down. This zone for a person is quite dangerous as a change that catches you unguarded is always detrimental. That's why in history we have learned that the rulers would safeguard their kingdom with an army of warriors against potential attack from the enemy. But in your life, you are the sole warrior and no one will safeguard it for you.

In this book, I am sharing my journey of unexpected change and how at one point my life came spiraling down with events beyond my control. It was only when I learned to derive the learning out of these situations, did I see the manifestation in a different light. Life had forced some tacit lessons on me, and it was for me to choose between giving up or making up with life. Just like how the tectonic plates in the earth's crust shift when heat is generated from the radioactive process, the shift in our life also happens as a result of hidden elements that do not serve your life's purpose, like in my case my past emotional baggage.

This is when I also realized that life goes spiraling down more due to the internal conflicts and struggles than the external circumstances that we call as "unexpected." Very rarely is the topic of "internal struggle" referred to as the core reason for the problem in life. But if you carefully look back at your experiences in life, it is your emotions like ego, anger, and regret that have played the villain in worsening the situation. It has less to do with failed judgments or wrong decisions as they are merely occurrences that shall pass one day. What makes matters worse is your incapacity to handle your inner self. The main aspect of this book is the role of emotional intelligence in managing change. A positive or negative outcome of any circumstance is a consequential evidence of how well we manage change.

I have narrated my own experiences to derive the learnings, which at that point I was unaware of. This would perhaps inspire you to also look at your own life and bring out the hidden lessons creating the "aha" moments.

I am a Woman . . . A tribute to all women out there!

I am a Woman, multifaceted creation of God,
I am also referred to as a Daughter, Sister, Wife,
and a Mother.
I have the strength to bear a child and the sorrows of life.
I feel the joy in spreading happiness around me and
standing strong in times of need.
Strength and courage are my soul mates,
with whose support I tread this long journey of life.

I am not weak as I have the courage to defeat the
challenges of life.
I am forgiving by nature, but this is not my weakness,
it is my beautiful thought of love.
With respect I embark on the journey of life but often
am expected to sacrifice in return,
not complaining about the harsh moments of life, but
I embrace every moment with love.

Deep thoughts flow inside me wondering,
has God created woman for a purpose?
Leaving me in doubt when the world abuses this
wonderful creation.

BACK IN CONTROL

Then I gather strength to stand up tall,
but brought on my knees when the unfortunate
makes me fall.
My belief and strength turn tired and frail and
seek some consoling moments,
but is hard to find when the inevitable takes its place.

With love and affection, I was reared by my family so dear,
but crushed to death by the world that fails to
stand by me here.
You will not emerge strong by seizing away my sanity,
I am an achiever in thoughts and deeds, and the
world now salutes me for this.

The world cannot be a better place without
me as it would be a heart devoid of soul,
but I do not long to be with you without respect
from your soul.
I am who I am and will always emerge strong,
after all I am a Woman whose strength is impossible
to be challenged at all.

—Jyothika Shetty

Chapter 1
Emotional Intelligence and the Leader in You

For Leaders, the first task in management has nothing to do with leading others: step one poses the challenge of knowing and managing oneself.

—Daniel Goleman

EMOTIONAL INTELLIGENCE OR EI is the ability to understand and manage your own emotions and also of people around you. A person who is emotionally intelligent is able to understand how they feel and react in different circumstances, the meaning of these emotions, and how it can affect people around them. In our day-to-day life too EI plays an important role as this helps us to build relationships, make decisions with clarity, maintain emotional balance, and also have a positive outlook in life. The majority of the problems we face in life are self-induced, and this is understood only when we are able to think with clarity.

In leadership, being emotionally intelligent is extremely important as the success rate of a leader with high EI is much better than a person who has a low EI. No one wants to work with a boss who is always stressed and reactive. A boss who is calm and pragmatic receives the highest support from his team. He is the one who is also able to find solutions to problems as he has the capacity to assess the situation before reacting.

Daniel Goleman, an American psychologist, was instrumental in popularizing the concept of emotional intelligence. According to him, an emotionally intelligent person is skilled in four areas: identifying emotions, using emotions, understanding emotions, and regulating emotions. A person who is able to practice these key skills is able to handle life in a much better manner. This also becomes the key to their success in all aspects of life as they are able to think clearly and respond dearly.

The term leader or leadership may immediately draw your attention to people leading an organization, but in all these years I have understood that leadership is an act; it is what you make out of a given situation. You can be a leader in your daily life and inspire people through your actions. It is the perspective that one develops from the success and failures that are faced. It is not a winning formula that is applied from day one because it is a continuous process that is tried and tested and modified along the way. If you take every failure as a learning, then you naturally position your mind to see things differently; but if you find the shortcomings in every success, then any business concept will seem inadequate. Therefore, leadership is an experience; it is a journey of allowing yourself to attempt, make mistakes, and learn from them.

When the term leader is used in this book it does not refer to leaders in an organization. Leadership is a quality that is present in all of us and is useful in all walks of life. A leader is the one who inspires others to take charge of their life and responsibilities for a bigger purpose. But before doing that one has to be able to lead and inspire their own life to pull them out of the dark and create a life that is nothing short of a miracle. Everyone in their own capacity is a leader because a leader is the one who inspires others to believe in themselves. The world has seen many leaders so far in various fields, from political to business, spiritual to science. Despite their different levels of achievement, they are all respected because they have inspired people in some way or the other. In other words, they have a few unique traits that make them leaders.

This means that a leader is the one who inspires and not necessarily someone who is a head of an organization. Every known leader started as a thought leader with a purpose more than intention. The purpose to achieve what they believed in and not with an intention to be a leader. Their actions eventually made them a leader as it started inspiring people to think differently and take action, thus creating a leader within them. This means there is a leader in each one of you, and several leadership lessons are hidden in your life experience. The only difference is that we often underestimate the potential of our story and do not share it with others. If you develop an attitude of finding lessons in every chapter of your life that we can use to create our own life, wouldn't it be great?

In the traditional sense, leadership concepts are often derived by reading books and from formal education. While this is a good way to introduce ourselves to the concept, the impact is created when you end up practicing it. Obviously, they are learned by trial and error which cannot be avoided nor ignored. The question is, how can these be learned and applied in our own lives?

Leadership is a vast concept and includes many traits that culminate into a good leader. These traits are learned through conscious awareness and continuous practice. But no one is perfect, and thus learning becomes a lifelong pursuit of becoming a better version of ourselves. But learning becomes easier and effective when you learn to understand yourself better and the way you react to situations. Being aware of your environment and how and why people react the way they do helps you strengthen the way you think and react to situations. When you attain this awareness, you become capable of aligning your thoughts and actions in a way that helps build a powerful you. This awareness in technical terms is called **Emotional Intelligence.**

> *If your emotional abilities aren't in hand, if you don't have self-awareness, if you are not able to manage your distressing emotions, if you can't have empathy and have*

effective relationships, then no matter how smart you are, you are not going to get very far.

—Daniel Goleman

Lessons are not those that are learned and forgotten but those that help define our future thinking and action. When we are weighed down by the debris of fear and worries of life the easiest way out is to give up—some give up hope, and a few, their life. But what we need to think deeply is, why does one really give up their life? From what I have understood, the fear of facing reality is the main reason one gives up. Until you have not committed a fraud or a crime, there is absolutely no reason to worry. Every problem has a solution, and if we have the courage to face it and find solutions, every problem can be solved over time.

Everyone is a leader, and it is when you learn these lessons can you bring a rational approach toward anything you do in life. A leader who finds it hard to handle emotions will not be able to make balanced decisions at work. Similarly, when our thoughts are not aligned with the purpose there is a constant struggle between the mind and the heart. We end up making decisions that may create more trouble in our lives and sour relationship with others. But when you are able to understand the emotions that you are going through and the possible outcome, you will be able to rewire the brain and the thoughts to create a better outcome.

Have you noticed a few people who are cool in every situation? Upon observing them it seems like they are in control of the situation and that too with a smile on their face. Chances are that they are what psychologists refer to as emotionally intelligent. Emotional intelligence is the ability to understand and handle our own emotions as well as understand others' emotions. It is a known fact that our intelligence has a big role to play in our success, and research says that being emotionally intelligent helps us achieve this success. Emotional intelligence helps right from decision-making to building the right attitude.

> In a study of skills that distinguish star performers in every field from entry-level jobs to executive positions, the single most important factor was not IQ, advanced degrees, or technical experience, it was EQ. Of the competencies required for excellence in performance in the job studies, 67 percent were emotional competencies.
>
> —Daniel Goleman

The importance of emotional intelligence was apparent when "CareerBuilder" conducted a national survey with more than 2600 hiring managers and human resource professionals in the year 2011. It was found that 59% of hiring managers said they would not hire someone with high IQ but low EI and 75% said that employees with high emotional intelligence are more likely to be promoted.

Multiple studies and reports have shown that people with high emotional intelligence handle a wide range of challenging situations with grace. They perform well (1) in conflict resolution, (2) in cooperating with people from diverse backgrounds and skill sets, and also (3) under pressure.

This is possible since emotional intelligence deals with the following quintessential components of personality.

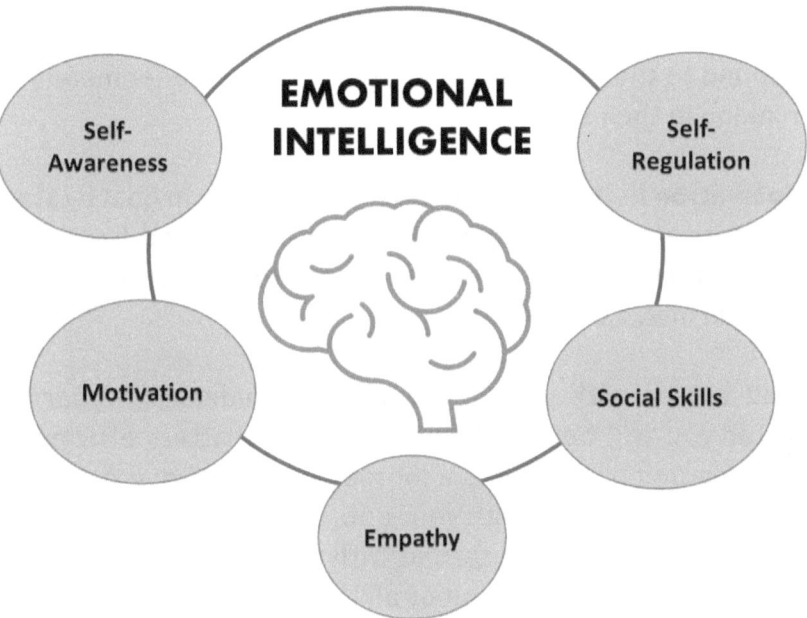

Self-Awareness is where when you recognize and understand your own emotions and are able to understand the effect of your mood, actions, as well as the emotions of other people.

Self-Regulation is when you know when to use your emotions. You go through the emotions you feel, but you express them only at the right time.

Social Skills is developing the ability to interact well with others. This goes one step beyond understanding others. Here you also understand to use the right emotions to interact with others.

Empathy is the ability to understand others' emotions and why are they behaving the way they are. It helps you to respond to their behavior in an appropriate manner merely by thinking in their shoes.

Motivation helps you to achieve your long-term goal by staying motivated. The benefit of staying motivated here goes beyond materialistic gains and is based on staying passionate to fulfill internal needs and gains.

It all begins with you, and when you understand yourself better you will be able to handle other matters efficiently. Understanding yourself is a journey and not a one day's job. It also has a lot to do with your upbringing and the emotional baggage that you have carried with you all these years. Your emotions are a culmination of all these years you have spent on this earth, and to understand and regulate them will take time and concerted effort. But the mantra here is practice, practice, and practice. Every experience if considered as a lesson learned will lead to various explorations of possibilities that will help you remain in control.

Chapter 2
The Yolk in the Egg

No story is perfect, but find that perfect lesson which makes your story worth sharing.

"JYOTHIKA! PLEASE COME to see me," said my ninth-grade class teacher while watching me through the iron rods of the class window. She was upset that I was not on my best behavior after I had just given my exams. She complained that I was talking too loudly while the exams in the other class were still in progress.

"Yes Ma'am," I said and walked up the stairs and reached the classroom, while she was waiting for me. I entered the classroom, and she asked me to sit in front of her.

After a minute of silence, the teacher said, "Look at your cousin." My cousin, who was like my own sister, was one year older than me, and we lived together in the same house. She was a studious child whose voice was hardly heard, quite contrary to me who believed in being heard.

"Why can't you be like her?" she continued. After a pause, I opened my right-hand fist, looked at my fingers, and replied, "Ma'am, the fingers in my hand are not of the same size so how could I be like her?"

> **No one can make you feel inferior without your permission.**

Looking back at this incident I still wonder why my teacher never said anything after this. But this is a preview to the kind of child I was. Someone who never held back her opinion and did not believe in standing in the grey zone. It was either black or white because of which I always got into arguments easily.

Comparison is the key reason for creating negative self-image, especially among children. It leaves a lasting impression in the minds which affects them in their adult life. Our limiting belief is also the result of how our environment has treated us without us being fully aware. Constant reinforcement of others' opinion about us leads to a self-fulfilling prophecy where we as an individual begin to conform to the expectation of the person with a false opinion.

I certainly gave a hard time to boys in my locality who never attempted to enter into an argument with me. This was probably the reason why my cousins pushed me to handle the arduous task of switching off the television while a bunch of kids continued to watch the game of cricket in our house.

The Growing Up Years
The television was introduced to us in the late 1980s, and this came as a prized possession as not everyone could buy one at that time. Ours was one of the few households that owned a television in our locality, and therefore, the kids in the neighborhood would flock to our house to watch their favorite serial, the mythological series on a Sunday morning, or the Bollywood melody on a Saturday evening. Ours was a black-and-white TV, and it was the fanciest electronic gadget that we had at that point. Our house seemed like a modern mini home theater, not because of the size of the TV but due to the size of the crowd that would squeeze themselves on the floor in our fairly spacious hall.

Imagine switching off the TV when so many pairs of eyes are glued to that tiny little screen? I could perhaps credit the undying spirit in me which must have scared those innocent little children. Looking back at those moments I can proudly say that my childhood with my three cousins were the best days of my life. I grew up in a household of nine people, as ours was a joint family, and I was under the care of my grandmother. My mother's older sister and her family also lived together, and she was instrumental in bringing me up and giving me a beautiful childhood. If there is one thing that I credit my aunty, it is for not conditioning my thoughts and giving me the creative freedom and confidence to be me. Perhaps this is the reason why she pursued her love for dancing as a voluntary teacher in our school. My vivid memories of her teaching folk dance to us during our school programs still remain fresh in my mind.

The Positive Influencers

One day after class hours, she was training a group of children in the school. I had to wait for her in silence since I would go back home with my aunt. That day I felt so sad because I was not a part of the group dance. I was possessive because I was not willing to share my aunt's attention, who I fondly call "Mummy," with the other children. I held back my tears and did not show that I was not in favor of her rendering voluntary service to others.

> Have at least one positive influencer, at all times, in your life as they are the ones who motivate you to stay on the right path.

While my aunty was soft and tender, my grandma was the one who ruled the whip. Coming from a family background that follows the matriarchal lineage, my grandmother was a prominent personality in our family. She was a landlady and was well known and respected in the family as well as in our neighborhood. She would never get intimidated by the strongest of men nor did she overstep the behavioral etiquette of societal norms back then. She led a balanced life and at the same time instilled strength in each one of us.

My grandmother has been the biggest influencer in my life. Her leadership qualities have been instilled in me as an inherent trait. Positive influencers play a major role in transforming the soft YOLK IN THE EGG to a healthy chick through their wisdom and action, preparing us to withstand the realities of life. This I understood much later in life, but this is also when I understood that our emotional and mental state of mind in the later years of our life is directly connected to the experiences we go through as children. Although the state of mind in our youth is camouflaged under the debris of responsibility, aspiration, and worldly affairs, the consequences get triggered once we start becoming aware of our purpose in life.

Developing Self-Image

I remember my grandmother being particular about the type of people we moved along with. By this, I mean that she would avoid people who would be deterrents to our confidence-building process, people who would talk negatively in our presence. This has been the key foundation to building my personality and self-esteem. Parents often do not realize that it is crucial for them to protect their young ones from people who may pass negative comments about the child. Some of my friends have had experiences where their skin color would be compared to that of their mothers'. These comments may not necessarily be deliberate but could affect the self-confidence of a child. But once this is realized, it is important that a parent makes a deliberate effort to avoid such a company to protect the child's self-image. This also teaches the child to trust the parent in every way. Although I had a generation gap with my grandmother, my cousins and I shared a special bond with her because my grandmother stood by us always. She was particularly concerned about me as I was under her guardianship since my parents had followed the shores of the gulf in the late 1970s.

> **Respect yourself first; you are your biggest cheerleader.**

Much earlier in life, I learned that one has to look beyond the petty matters by indulging in positive communication. In order to grow one has to make a conscious effort to be with people who will uplift you and not pull you down, whether it is friends or family. Also, these are the people who help you look beyond the petty matters. When your actions are a result of positive thoughts, then you accumulate positive karma, which influences your life at large.

Learning to Be Independent
"Oh! The crow has taken my mom away," said the 6-year-old me, as I watched my mother board the Mumbai-bound flight as she was traveling to Dubai for the first time in 1981. Those days the Mangalore airport did not handle international flights, and overseas flights could only be accessed from the nearest international airport, which we did from erstwhile Bombay. Probably this was the reason why I was fascinated with being an air hostess and aspired to be one as I was growing up. It is a different story that I later wanted to be a lawyer, probably owing to my ability to call a spade a spade. Looking back at the oscillating career aspirations, this certainly was the process of my transformation just like the *yolk in the egg*. I must admit that very early in my life I had learned to go with the flow. Although much of my growing years I lived away from my parents, this taught me to adapt to situations and live in the present moment.

Telephones those days were a luxury, and we did not get our connection for eight long years after booking. I would run to my neighbor's house when my parents would call to talk to me. Once a month my mother resorted to writing lengthy letters to me which were a joy to read. I responded to the letters with the same enthusiasm, and probably this is the reason I developed an interest in writing much earlier in life. This was not evident until I reached my senior secondary school. I realized that it was during those times that the traces of traits that showed up as a child were actually the life-changing opportunities that would yield to me one day. Maybe this is the reason why I was an outstanding student in subjects like political science and history.

But how many of us take the time to seriously look at those bouts of natural traits that keep showing up now and then? Much of the lost opportunity lies in our formative years when we or our parents fail to identify our strengths. We either do not receive support or are asked to pursue something that stood at par with the societal norms. I too was naive and whatever I did was never planned, but I must admit that it was impulsive. This is the reason why I ended up making decisions that were not agreeable to others but perfectly suited my fiery sign, like quitting college even before I understood what college truly meant. Whether they were planned or not, I focused less on the root cause and more on the result. When the rest of the children lived with their parents, I lived away from mine. When my friends shared memories of planning their future after consulting their parents, I grew up even before I finished my childhood. *Much of my growing years are hidden in the creases of the lengthy letters that my mom and I wrote to each other.*

> **When mistakes occur, redirect the energy.**

A New World

"Come in, let me give you a hug," said my dad seated in a bus as my parents were returning to Dubai via Mumbai after a month-long vacation.

"No, I will not do it. I don't want to be taken by this bus," I said. I was referring to my fear of being driven by the bus with my parents once I got in. It was apparent that I was comfortable living away from my parents and did not miss them much, or at least that is what I thought.

My ability to be independent was put to test much earlier in life when I embarked on a flight to Dubai as an unaccompanied minor in the year 1985. I stepped on the shores of Dubai as a 10-year-old child, and this was an unforgettable experience. Dubai was witnessing a metamorphosis of change, and our paths crossed at a time when the city was getting ready for this paradigm shift. After my vacation, I came back with a bagful of stories and narrated them to my cousins and friends, something that I was proud of.

Some of the life-changing decisions in my life have been made in an impulsive manner. They worked in my favor, though not because they were right, but I am sure things could have been done differently. However, they turned out to be right only because of my attitude to focus on positive results. One such incident was my decision to quit college halfway and join my parents. In the early 1990s, I decided to quit college because I was not happy when my father shifted me to his aunt's house. Since I was used to living with my cousins, I was not willing to adapt to this new life. This was my way of revolting as a teenager.

> **Decisions are not always meant to be made alone. There is nothing wrong with reaching out for advice.**

Quite clearly there have been a few moments in my life that have been life-changing, and quitting college was the first of those moments that changed the direction of my life significantly.

I may not recommend this to you, but I certainly do not regret this decision for a simple reason that it gave me some precious moments before embarking on yet another life-changing moment. An unexpected turn of events that was about to open my eyes to a completely new world where I was a stranger. Many decisions had to be made in a short period of time, and all I could do was trust my capabilities to do the best with the available resources.

When things don't go as expected it is best to go with the flow as it becomes easier to accept change. Maybe it is much easier when you are trying to make a life for yourself. But the question is—is it easier to go with the flow when you have a lot at stake? This is where the real struggle begins.

Keys to Understanding Yourself

1. No one can make you feel inferior with your permission.
2. Have at least one positive influencer, at all times, in your life as they are the ones who motivate you to stay on the right path.
3. Respect yourself first; you are your biggest cheerleader.
4. When mistakes occur, redirect the energy.
5. Decisions are not always meant to be made alone. There is nothing wrong with reaching out for advice.

Your actions after reading this chapter
The first step toward being emotionally intelligent is to be aware of your emotions and your reaction in different situations. If you are going through a rough patch and want to declutter your mind, then this book will serve as a great tool to align your thoughts and find solutions.

After reading this chapter you will begin to realize that everyone's story has two sides, one what happens to you and second what you make out of it. Some of the simple lessons are hidden between the fine lines of the narratives that are relevant to each one of us. This chapter will encourage you to look at your own life and search for those lessons which you have not found so far. Start by journaling your thoughts and experience on a daily basis. The best leadership lessons are not found in business schools but in your own life experience.

After reading this chapter you may wonder how you will find the lessons in your life. This begins by observing every aspect of your life and following these steps:

1. Create a timeline of your experience; for example, group your experience between the age group of 5 and 10, 11 and 15, and so on.
2. Note down every little detail and find the elements that connect with you. Also, note the characters in the incident and the dialogues that you remember.
3. Begin with the end in mind and see what purpose you want to serve by deriving these lessons. Align your

perspective with your purpose when you are identifying the learnings.

• • •

Check Your Emotional Intelligence Score
You may want to check your emotional intelligence level before you proceed with this book. There are multiple tests available online, but I found the following website information to be simple and straightforward: https://www.arealme.com/eq/en/

While different sources interpret the scores in different ways, an average score is considered to be between 75 and 150, and anything over 150 is a perfect score.

• • •

Chapter 3
Emotional Intelligence in Decision-Making

Smart decisions require emotions. Far from interfering with rationality, the absence of emotion and feeling can break down rationality and make wise decision-making almost impossible.

—Antonio Damasio (Professor of Neuroscience at the University of Southern California)

IMAGINE YOU HAVE to make a decision that could impact your life significantly. Look at this picture, and for a moment think of it as the door to your future. You have several options that look similar, yet each of them has something unique to offer. The question is, which door will you choose?

Every time you make a decision, the other option draws you to its side, restarting the game again. How frustrating is that?

Image: Arek Socha from Pixabay

Someone must have even suggested, "Follow your heart." Do you think this is the best way to make a decision? Or maybe you should consult someone experienced or weigh the pros and cons. The advice that your heart would give would be based on your past experience and emotions that could steer it in the wrong direction. It also has much to do with social conditioning, cultural norms, and way of living. Any decision based only on emotions could potentially have a detrimental consequence.

Take anger, for example; where fear breeds uncertainty, anger instills confidence. Anger makes people undertake risks and underestimate the risk associated with it. This is where one could go wrong in overestimating their capacity to deal with a high-risk situation and end up hurting themselves. Thus, decisions made under the extremities of emotions can lead to bad decision-making.

Researchers at Cornell University estimated that an average adult makes about 226.7 decisions each day on food alone. As responsibility increases, the multitude of decisions you have to make also increases. The internet, however, claims that an average adult makes about 35,000 remotely conscious decisions every day, which is an astonishing number. Although we have no means to validate this number, imagine how many decisions possibly end up being right. Some decisions have a greater impact on our lives and are not always easy to make. Decision-making, thus, is a skill that needs to be developed over time by first understanding what influences our current decisions.

What Is It That Helps Us to Make Good Decisions?
According to a 2014 research by Harvard University on Emotions and Decision-Making concluded that emotions constitute powerful and predictable drivers of decision-making.

Therefore, the life that you are living today is also due to the emotional decisions you have made in the past. Feeling of anger or happiness is temporary, and any decision made at this time is bound to change your opinion later. Some of the impulsive decisions that I have made in my life were under the influence of negative experiences triggered by emotions such as anger, frustration, and sadness. Similarly, not all decisions made under the influence of positive emotion were the best decisions of my life. The only difference is that even if the decisions were made under negative emotion, I tried to make it work for me. But such a method is time-consuming and tiring. It may not give you the optimum results that a well-thought decision could possibly give. Therefore, good decisions come with certain conscious actions that we take without the influence of unrelated emotions.

People who are emotionally intelligent don't remove all emotions from their decision-making. They remove emotions that have nothing to do with the decision.

—Prof. Côté, University of Toronto

A person makes a good decision not because they are the smartest but because they have allowed themselves to experience all of it. It is only when you experience emotions can you eliminate the ones that have nothing to do with the decision. A conscious decision to identify the emotional triggers and the ability to work on them will only help you make good decisions.

Some people who analyze the situation well try to not let emotions come in the way of their decision-making. But emotions provide us with the required stimulation to make decisions, and there is no denying that emotions build relationships. It is the very reason that this world is what it is today, good or bad. During the stressful period of COVID-19, the best of the best practical thinkers could not stay away from feeling worried, scared, and nervous. The financial market crashed with never-ending bad news, making investors nervous and resulting in emotion-based decisions.

So, what is the best advice that can be given to a decision-maker? The first step would be to accept that you are going to have emotions, but keep them from influencing your thoughts. While one cannot avoid emotions, we can certainly manage them to make good decisions. Clearly, there is no art in decision-making but being emotionally intelligent could

EMOTIONAL INTELLIGENCE IN DECISION-MAKING

prove to be an effective tool. If you have to make a burning decision that is worrying you, then you could *first wait before reacting*.

Imagine, you learned from your client that your best friend has approached him with a counter product that your company offers. Having insight into your price list and quality, he has been able to design his proposal with a competitive advantage. This obviously puts you in a difficult situation, and you are ruminating your next course of action.

But wait a moment. Before making a decision, you can go through the following process:

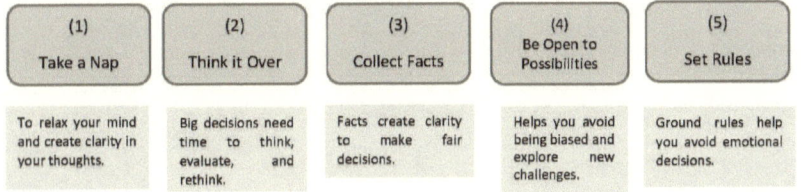

(1) Take a Nap	(2) Think it Over	(3) Collect Facts	(4) Be Open to Possibilities	(5) Set Rules
To relax your mind and create clarity in your thoughts.	Big decisions need time to think, evaluate, and rethink.	Facts create clarity to make fair decisions.	Helps you avoid being biased and explore new challenges.	Ground rules help you avoid emotional decisions.

I cannot claim that I have been always aware of my emotions. For me, this has been more a work in progress, and each day I am understanding myself better. When I look back, I certainly see that I have covered a long journey which has helped me shape my personality. The impulsive decisions I have made may not be the best of the decisions of my life but have proved to be great learning curves. My learnings have helped me improve my relationships with family and friends and how I communicated and dealt with them. We are all human beings and emotional outbursts are bound to happen, but the frequency and intensity with which an outburst happens is now aligned with my thought and is manageable. My mantra to understanding myself better is experiencing my emotion and growing through the process. If we can understand ourselves better, we can deal with our situations and make better decisions.

Chapter 4
The Fork in the Road

*Good decisions come from experience, and
experience comes from bad decisions.*

THROUGHOUT LIFE, WE face situations when we have to make that difficult decision about something in our life. When we have more than one option, the decision-making gets even tougher, especially when it impacts our life greatly. We end up worrying, which one is the right option? What if the other option was better? The never-ending "ifs" and "buts" lead us to anxiety and worry. Thus, when one stands in between two roads not able to decide which road to take, you face *The Fork in the Road*.

Look back to learn and not regret.

The anxiety of missing out on the best result further propels the intensity, creating uncertainty and fear in a person. What does one do when such a situation stares at you? Have you ever thought about what could be the best possible way to deal with such a situation? In reality, there is no best way to deal with such a situation. Some choose to seek help, whereas some prefer to trust their instincts or go with the flow. I am one of those who belong to the latter tribe because I have always done what *feels* right.

Whether you are a student who is deciding your field of study, a woman who is contemplating the right time to get back to work after delivery, or a man who is torn between staying put as an employee and starting his own business, whatever the reason may be, one has to make a decision anyway. So, what's the big deal? Life does not come with a manual, but you have to just make it work. Whatever decision you take—one thing you have to know is you shouldn't look back with regret.

In my life, I have never had a Plan B, not because I was overconfident about destiny but because I trusted myself and my ability to work hard. I always believed that if you trust yourself and your ability to work hard, then luck finds its way to your door. Taking action for me was more important than weighing the result because if you make a sincere effort then results are bound to happen.

But this time it was my chance to face the "Fork in the Road," because the situation was such that it was bound to turn another major chapter in my life. If I had to list down those defining moments in my life, I would certainly list this event as a moment that changed the direction of my life.

Moments I Cherished
After I quit college, I joined my parents in Dubai permanently. I was a happy soul because a lot had been missed over all these

years away from them. In August 1992, I turned 17, and this was the first time I celebrated my birthday with my parents. My father was so excited that he called our friends to join the celebration. I felt like a queen and was treated like one. On the morning of my birthday, I went to the beauty salon to get myself ready for the celebration, and a buffet dinner was arranged at home with a beautiful cake that had my pet name "Pinky" carved on it. I even applied henna on my palms that made me look elegant and pretty. I felt on the top of the world as my dad became the wind beneath my wings.

> *Patience, preparation, and practice are the essentials in building your decision-making capability.*

Subsequently, I experienced many such moments of irreplaceable joy, and one of them was when I got my driving license even before I completed 21 years of age. Getting a driving license in Dubai those days was an arduous task with several attempts that were filled with rejection and disappointment. My dad arranged practice classes for thirty continuous days, after which I was permitted to give a test. He insisted that I attend these classes prior to attempting any test, as he did not want me to rush on getting the license. He got his own driving instructor to train me for one whole month and by the end of my thirtieth session, I was confident with the skill I had attained. Obviously, there was no escaping here because the driving instructor would closely monitor my moves and he would report to my dad immediately. I had to be regular and on time, and one hour of rigorous driving put my focus on my end goal.

I was a fast learner, and at the tender age of 20 I picked up my driving lessons too quickly. At the first attempt of my road test, the assessor watched me drive and smiled. I was certain that he was quite impressed with my driving and I had passed my test. After a while he said, "I see that your driving is good, but you are too young to pass your first test. Please come again."

I was not too impressed with him, but the fact that he appreciated my driving skills stuck in my mind and worked as a self-motivator. I finally cleared the test in the third attempt and that too just within three months. It was time for another celebration, and my dad was hysterical; perhaps he clearly understood the pain behind getting a license and that too this fast. He once again called for a celebration and boasted about his daughter's accomplishment to our circle of friends. These were the moments I cherished as I would have never experienced this if I had continued to live away from my parents.

> **Look for positives in any situation as they are great motivators.**

To achieve anything in life one has to prepare well because it is only then you build your confidence to face failures and learn to trust yourself. I did not understand when my father insisted that I took 30 days of continuous classes before attempting the test. When I lost the first two attempts, I realized that the training was my dad's way of building patience in me and inculcating the value of practice and patience. My dad also taught me that celebrating these little moments of achievement is an important part of the whole journey. Human beings are often so stuck up with their end goal that they fail to recognize the little milestones that we cross in order to get there and also celebrate it. The moments of enjoyment were my dad's way of celebrating those little achievements that were major milestones in my life.

The Wind Beneath My Wings

My father was an emotional person, and even if I fell sick, he would be in tears, and that taught me that crying is not a sign of weakness but a powerful way to live in the present moment.

> Don't be afraid to show your weakness in any form. Vulnerability means you are touching lives.

My father was a handsome man with a larger-than-life personality. He had great mathematical ability, which explains his strong business acumen. He was a navy cadet during his school days and was chosen to represent our Karnataka state to meet the second President of India, Dr. Sarvepalli Radhakrishna. He kept boasting about this privilege, which only made me proud each time he narrated the story. I would enjoy hearing his childhood stories that were filled with Robinhood moments. He was also quite well known for his boisterous behavior as he was fearless and was ready to face any kind of challenge. At the same time a hard-working person whom I always looked up to.

My most memorable moments those days were when my parents used to visit India during their annual vacation. He had this charisma that gave me an impression of a dependable and tough man. I was always happy when my dad was around me. Although my dad moved to Dubai when I was barely two years old, I had a special attachment to him and could never ever think of a life without him.

He had a dream and his dream was to own a restaurant. When I was an infant, my dad owned a small restaurant in my name, and my mom was a key stakeholder in the business. But when my father decided to move from our small town of erstwhile Mangalore, seeking greener pastures, he decided to close this business. Years later when I was cleaning our storeroom, I found a name board that had my name on it. I was ecstatic and asked my aunty about this name board. This was when my aunty told me the entire story of my father's stint in the restaurant business. No wonder the restaurant business was something that ran in my dad's DNA, and it was his much-cherished dream.

Unfortunately, he could never realize this dream for several reasons that were beyond his control. Those days when he moved to the Gulf with my mother, life was not the same. The Gulf countries were just gaining momentum economically, and the influx of expatriates in the country was on the rise. People who came during those initial stages had to face the heat of the sand dunes that were in abundance while the concrete structures were still not in place. In a way, I can proudly say that the generation of my parents has been a part of the growth story of Dubai.

Back then he was associated with the restaurant business, if not owning one. His ultimate dream was to set up his own business, and along the way, he tried his hands on some other businesses. Ultimately these businesses failed and also brought a lot of unrest in our life. During all those years my mother was his rock. She stood by him through thick and thin, whatever the situation was. After all, they were childhood sweethearts. He was financially broken, which drained much of his positive traits under the blanket of uncertainty. When I moved to Dubai, my dad was in his recovery stage, and I came as a fresh breath of energy in his life. My parents found a purpose to move on in life and were extremely happy with me around. Until then they had not experienced what it is to have a child in the house who was as talkative as me.

We make a lot of sacrifices in life for future pleasures that are unseen. Circumstances sometimes do not permit us to follow our heart, but it is not always that we do not have a choice. It is that we do not want to take a chance to make that choice. When my parents faced the Fork in the Road to take me with them or not, the choice was obviously the latter. The decision was influenced by the Plan B that they had which was my grandma to take care of me in India. If that safety net was not there then I would be probably sharing more memories of my parents with you. What I am trying to establish here is that everyone faces the Fork in the Road, but having too many choices sometimes dilutes our spirit. You have to understand that whatever the choice, ultimately, success is based on your indomitable spirit to make it work.

The Growing Distance
While my dad was my force and pride, my mother was the one who took good care of me. She was a good-hearted person but with a high temperament. While I was at ease with my dad, I had to be extra cautious with my mom and watch my mischief. One of the reasons I hesitated to get close to my mom was because I was scared of her. My dad was soft-spoken and would never shout at me. I knew I would be excused even if I made a mistake, but with my mother, there was no excuse. When I was a teenager my mother would tell me how to dress up as she had a good sense of style, but I must confess that it did not suit the style of a teenager. We often got into arguments because

of our varied choice of clothes, and my dad would be dragged into the conversation to find a solution. I would secretly walk up to my dad and ask him to talk to my mom and explain to her to avoid telling me what to wear. These were the typical problems that a teenager usually faces with her mother.

However, underneath these simple problems lay a greater and deeper sense of distance that I did not comprehend at that time. *"Tallying the balance sheet of life"* refers to the deeper issues that I had to deal with later in my life. My mother was more like a visitor for me who I saw perhaps once in two years. Although she tried a lot later in life to fix the issue, it was certainly too late. There seemed like there was no way out as the impression had managed to capture the depth of my heart and it was meant to stay there for a very long time. This is when I told my father that I would never send my kids away from me and would look after them on my own. I was barely 16 years old, and my thought process clearly reflected the person deep inside me. What I expressed was misconstrued as my rebellious nature and not the thoughts that harbored as a result of my awareness of my emotions.

In a Blink of a Second
It was the year 2004, when the world witnessed a devastating incident—the tsunami that killed over two hundred thousand people and changed life for many. This came at a time when people were not prepared and took everyone by surprise. It also changed the lives for many, but eventually, all those who survived the unfortunate event did learn to move along with their lives. Did they complain about what happened? I am sure they did, and they had all the right to do so because they lost their

loved ones in a blink of a second. These were defining moments that changed the direction of their life, but what mattered was the way each one of them managed to rebuild their lives.

When the entire world witnessed this tsunami, I was just coming to terms with the tsunami that had taken place in my life. Eight years before this incident, I had turned 21, and this birthday was a bit different because my dad was traveling that day. Unlike my previous birthdays when he would make it the happiest moment for me, this one was quiet and receding. My father was traveling to India to attend to an urgent matter related to his health. Before he stepped out of the house, he ate his favorite sweet that was on the table saying, "Who knows, this could be my last one."

My mom and I were not nervous as it was a small health issue that he was attending to and would be back in no time. He had even asked my mother not to accompany him as this would mean I would be all alone at home. After he reached India he was admitted to the hospital, and he kept updating me of the progress. While my mother and I were waiting for the surgery to finish, late evening we received a call that my dad had a heart attack and that he was in the intensive care unit. We booked our tickets in the first available flight which was only the next morning, and we had to spend that night hoping that nothing would go wrong.

> *When you face the worst in life always tell yourself, "This too shall pass."*

This was one night that I can never forget in my life as it seemed the longest and most dreadful nightmare in my life.

The next morning, we took the flight to India, and during our journey my mom and I prepared ourselves for the worst. It all seemed like people were hiding something from us, and we kept guessing the inevitable. As we reached home, our worst nightmare unfolded—my dearest dad was gone forever. All I saw was a stiff cold body that was wrapped in white cloth waiting for his beloved wife and daughter to bid goodbye.

The tsunami in our life had washed away the most precious person from our lives. All this in a blink of a second and we were not prepared for this. It all seemed too soon, and yet we had to endure. I had just turned 21 and in a week's time, my dad was gone. It seemed like opening a door into a dark room, not knowing where the switch was. The only option was to hold the walls and find my way through the room to find that switch. Imagine a situation when you lose the biggest support of your life, your cheerleader without whom you cannot fathom life. This is when your entire life flashes in front of your eyes, unfolding the fine lines between the major events of your life.

A few months preceding my dad's departure he had told me a few strange things that I did not understand at that time. It was as if he knew that it was time for him to leave. He had already visited the doctor in India a few times but did not tell us what actually was his condition. All he mentioned to me one day was, "Please take care of your mom while I am not there anymore."

It was only after his departure I realized that all this while my dad knew that he had to prepare me for the inevitable.

Rest in Peace, my Hero . . . you will remain in my heart forever

The Fork in the Road

After a few months that were rough for my mother and myself, there was one question that stared at us, "What next?"

I did not have the answers to the questions that popped up from time to time, but I was not one of those people who liked to dwell in doubt. After such an incident many would end up asking, "Why Me?"

But not once did I ask this question. If there was one thing that I had to do is make the best of what I had. But I was faced with the *Fork in the Road* where I had to decide to step out of my comfort zone and return to Dubai and wind my dad's business or stay with my mom sinking in sorrow.

From my archive of life-changing decisions, I was about to make another one that was clearly preparing to change the direction of my life. Deciding to go back was another life-changing decision that created the change because I chose to do it. Staying back in India probably would have led to a different direction, but I had priorities to deal with. When I decided to face the unknown my decision was based on what was the need of the hour—at that time it was to seek closure to a lot of things that we had left abruptly. I was prepared to do what seemed right, and I knew the rest would fall in place. Initially, I

> **Have open communication with someone you trust. Brilliant ideas are often the result of deep conversation.**

was not prepared to do this alone, but with my mom's support, I decided to travel all alone and take matters in my hand. Between the narratives of life experience, I had grown overnight and was now responsible for my life.

When faced with a situation of uncertainty it is best to choose what seems not only right but what seems to push you to the next level. It may not be within your comfort zone, but be rest assured that when you see progress you will want to do more. See what you choose is aligned with your value system as it will propel your faith and belief and will help you to stay committed.

When you face the Fork in the Road, consult your mentor, friend, guide, parents, or someone you trust. They help you look at the situation in a different light as they have been there and done it. You can gain a lot from their experience, and two minds bring a different perspective to a particular situation. When you make a well-informed move, you have much better clarity to deal with the situation than indulging in a nonchalant move of the pawn that could potentially perturb you for the rest of your life.

Keys to Facing the Fork in the Road

1. Look back to learn and not to regret.
2. Patience, preparation, and practice are the essentials in building your decision-making capability.
3. Look for positives in any situation as they are great motivators.
4. Don't be afraid to show your weakness in any form. Vulnerability means you are touching lives.

5. When you face the worst in life always tell yourself "This too shall pass."
6. Have open communication with someone you trust. Brilliant ideas are often a result of deep conversation.

• • •

Your actions after reading this chapter
When you face the Fork in the Road situation and are confused about what is the best decision to take then begin with asking yourself, "What is your ultimate goal in life?"

Sometimes you may think that putting yourself through hardship is the only way to achieve your goals. Trying to justify how much you deserve your goal just because you have worked hard for it is just telling the lion not to eat you just because you fed it once.

Life is simple yet unforgiving and only the smart ones get to see the bright side of life. "Smart" means someone who understands their priority and makes a well-informed decision and not someone who becomes a victim of the situation by letting the situation control them. No two decisions can yield the same result, and thus the result of your decision is always going to be different from the one you have foregone. Do not aim at selecting the best option, but instead focus on making the best with the chosen option.

What Next?
You could start by taking an online "Decision-Making skill test" that will help you understand your current decision-making capability.

The test is available at: https://www.mindtools.com/pages/article/newTED_79.htm

• • •

How Can I Improve My Decision-Making Capability?
Decision-making capability is much more than the ability to look at and analyze the problem. It is a continuous process of enhancing clarity in your mind by working on a few areas in your own life:

1. Bring some art and music into your routine.
2. Learn a new skill or language and challenge your brain.
3. Network with people of different age groups.
4. Introduce physical activity in your daily routine.
5. Learn to cook.
6. Be active on social media if you like that space.

• • •

Step-by-Step Approach to Reach a Practical Solution
When you face a Fork in the Road, the following steps could help develop clarity and reach a practical solution:

Step 1: Identify the problem, opportunity, or challenge.
Step 2: Write down the possible solutions that you can think of.
Step 3: Identify the benefits and costs associated with each solution.

Step 4: Pick the most suitable solution that would help. *Tip: Pick a decision that will help you progress to the next level.*
Step 5: Implement the solution.
Step 6: Review the impact of the decision and amend the course of action, as required.

• • •

Chapter 5
Emotional Intelligence and Attitude

If you want to change attitudes, start with a change in behavior.

—*Katharine Hepburn*

IF YOU HAD to rate yourself between 1 and 10 on a Likert scale to understand your effectiveness in implementing action, then what would the result reveal? But before that, pause for a while and see what are the areas that influence your action.

Is it your skill, your planning, or your attitude?

Most likely it is your attitude that determines the effectiveness of your action. Right attitude can help you align your action as per the plan, but an attitude that is not right could lead to a negative frame of mind that could affect any plan.

Attitude is the feeling that you have toward a person or thing in your mind. This has a lot to do with the way we are brought up, the values we are exposed to, and the mindset that we have developed as a result of these factors. Depending on these metrics a person may react to a certain situation in a positive or a negative manner.

Emotion works hand-in-hand with the cognitive process and the way we think about an issue or situation. Thus, behavior and attitude are closely linked with each other, and we develop these based on our emotional quotient. Although not all behaviors may turn into attitudes, one cannot ignore the fact that attitudes can influence the behavior of a person. A Carnegie Foundation report once cited that 85% of your success comes from your skills and attitude and only 15% from your technical knowledge. Your knowledge will help you get there but skills and attitude will keep you there.

Emotions play an important role both in the work and social life of individuals. They can precisely affect the antecedents of behaviors such as attitudes, attributions, and perceptions. This only reiterates the fact that emotions once again are the building block to the kind of attitude you will choose to have. Having said that attitude is not something that cannot be changed, and this is possible when you chose to manage your emotions well.

Like decision-making which we discussed earlier, it all begins with being aware of your own emotions and how to manage them. Emotional intelligence helps build the following competencies required for developing a good attitude:

- Maintaining focus
- Giving your best
- Being coachable
- Regulating your emotions
- Flexibility

We are all born with a certain attitude in life, and it takes a lot of trial and error to understand that attitudes are meant to be changed for the better. A good attitude leads you to the path of success and a bad attitude could be detrimental to your growth. In the case of an unexpected change, it is the right attitude that will help you overcome the hurdles. In my case, I cannot claim that I had the best attitude when I was young. I was temperamental, impulsive, and also spoke my mind. It was easy to get into arguments and have the last word, and this in turn affected me with long-term damages. It was difficult to build friendships or relationships. This was not evident when I was young, but when I became independent, I could witness the detrimental effect an attitude could have. I had to make a conscious decision to work on this area, but this did not happen till much later in life.

So, What Is Right Attitude?
I will try to articulate the meaning of right attitude through "The Starfish Story" adapted from "The Star Thrower" by Loren Eiseley (1907–1977).

Once upon a time, there was a wise man who used to go to the ocean to do his writing. He had a habit of walking on the beach before he began his work. One day, as he was walking along the shore, he looked down the beach and saw a human figure moving like a dancer. As he got closer, he noticed that the figure was that of a young man picking up small objects and throwing them into the ocean.

He came closer and asked, "May I ask, what are you doing here?"

The young man paused, looked up, and replied. "Throwing starfish into the ocean."

The man was intrigued by this response and asked the boy why he was throwing it.

The young boy replied, "If I don't throw them, they will die when the tide goes low."

The man found this silly and said, "Do you realize there are thousands of starfish here? How could you make a difference to all of them"?

At this, the young man bent down, picked up yet another starfish, and threw it into the ocean. As it met the water, he said, "*It made a difference for that one.*"

What I am trying to establish through this story is the power of right attitude. It takes a right attitude to do greater good to yourself and others. A right attitude helps you see possibilities in challenges, gain in pain, and hope in despair. After all, this is what is required when you face an unexpected change. It will help you lead through the situation and not just hope for things to happen.

> *Everything can be taken from a man but one thing: the last of human freedoms—to choose one's attitude in any given set of circumstances, to choose one's own way.*
>
> —Viktor E. Frankl

Now ask yourself what was your attitude when you faced a challenge in your life? Did you give up or get up?

Emotional Intelligence has a significant role to play in building up our attitude. Since emotion is the basis for everything you do, creating awareness of your emotions and managing them will also lead to managing a good attitude. To manage your attitude, you could begin by tracking your own *behavior*. This of course comes with practice and once you create awareness of your own emotion.

If I consider my behavior a few years ago, I would get angry quickly and cool down at the same speed. There were times when I would not talk for days to my husband for a silly reason. I would not think before expressing my varied emotions as a result of which I easily got into arguments with others. Lack of empathy toward others probably made me react without thinking.

Looking back, it is probably because of my emotional trauma and limited interaction that I maintained with people that I did not fully develop my empathy levels. This is where widening your network and knowing more people around will bring you face-to-face with a plethora of personalities that will help you calibrate your attitude. You will learn to interact and understand with people and thus develop your interpersonal skills, which is essential to developing yourself.

Mark Murphy, an organizational leadership expert and author of *Hiring for Attitude* conducted a study on 20,000 new hires and found out that 48% of them failed within 18 months. What was even more surprising was that 89% of the time new hires failed for attitudinal reasons and only 11% for the lack of skill. These attitudinal issues included a lack of coachability, low levels of emotional intelligence and motivation, and bad temperament.

Herb Kelleher, former Southwest Airlines CEO used to say, "We can change skill levels through training, but we can't change attitude" (*The Work-Life Equation* by William L. Maw).

It is not always that you can behave the way you want, and at one stage you will realize the implications of being impulsive. These implications will force you to introspect your behavior and work on it along the way. In the end, it is a journey of trial and error, but it is always better to understand and accept our weakness and be willing to work on it.

Chapter 6
Your Attitude Determines Your Altitude

You may not be able to control every situation and its outcome, but you can control your attitude and how you deal with it.

FOLLOWING MY DAD'S death in August 1996, I was finding ways to recover from the trauma. The only way I could recover fast is by keeping myself busy in India. I started off by enrolling for driving classes and a travel-and-ticketing course—believe me, those days air tickets were issued manually! By this, I thought, if I could not achieve the possibility of fulfilling my childhood dream of becoming an air hostess, I could at least get a few steps closer to my dream.

In this class, we had a bunch of fun-loving students who became my good friends in no time. It gave me a new lease of life, which helped me cope up with the trauma that I had just been through. We built some of the best memories in this class that are still fresh in my mind. One such memory is that of my final convocation day. It was a yearly tradition where the outgoing class would put up a show for the final award ceremony. The director was looking for a student who could take up the responsibility of handling this big event. One day she came up to me and said, "Jyothika, I want you to take charge of the convocation."

> **Continue your passion even when the going gets tough. It helps develop an action-oriented attitude.**

Without a doubt, I accepted this opportunity and started my preparation. I created a fashion show that was a runaway success because it was creative, fun, and full of life. It included everyone in the class, even the boy who hardly attended class. To everyone's surprise, this very boy was a showstopper and stole the show. Following this successful event, the director came up to me and said, "I knew you could do it, and that's why I assigned you with the responsibility."

I had also topped the class in that batch, and it was like the Phoenix rising from the ashes. In spite of the deep sadness inside me, this course had helped me live a few happy moments with a smile. I was unknowingly living by my life mantra *"Be the best in whatever you do."* It is this attitude that also helped me to develop an attitude where I was never in a race to prove myself, thus developing a confidence that could not be easily deterred.

Looking back, there are two lessons I learned from this experience. One is to never say no to opportunities of growth and learning; second, teamwork is essential to create a successful project. I could have refused the request since I had never done this before. But I took it as a challenge and learned along the way. I could never pull off this event without a team, and hence I took the support of my classmates who worked hard with me. There are reasons why people fail to take action and the most common ones are

1. I do not know how to do it (Procrastinator),
2. I am sure it won't be possible (Pessimist),
3. It cannot be done (Quitter),

Great businessmen like Sir Richard Branson exemplified the truth that lies in the importance of taking action. He once said, *"If somebody offers you an amazing opportunity but you are not sure you can do it, say yes—then learn how to do it later."*

My traits of handling unexpected changes were already evident, thanks to my attitude of adapting to change. But traits get accentuated when they are equipped with the right emotion which is the result of right state of mind. I was not there yet as I did not feel on the top of the world despite topping the class. The trauma of my Dad's death had managed to sink deep into my inner self, which did not let any other emotion make way to my heart. It seemed like I was dragging my feet with the load full of emotions tied to me that were in a furious fight to pull me down.

This was a poignant reminder of the unprecedented situation in my life. Minor tasks such as dressing up seemed like an arduous one. I was heading to something that I could not comprehend, but all I could feel was empty and sad. Nothing seemed to catch my eye and excite me, and I was like a rose that had lost its fragrance.

Turning a New Chapter of Life

I was completely against the idea of returning to Dubai alone, but I had to do it and there was no two ways about it. My dad had a small business, and there were employees waiting for direction. After a lot of discussion with my mother, we made a pact that I would return to Dubai, settle my dad's business, and return to India. This was the first time I was taking charge of important issues and that too at a tender age of 21. But not once did I doubt my capacity to do it because I never got into evaluating the pros and cons. All I knew was that I had to get it done somehow.

> Don't let the entire staircase overwhelm you. Just focus on that first step.

Looking back at these moments, I feel that my unconditional attitude helped me get the best out of any situation. This is where I also learned that sometimes ignorance is bliss. The more you dig into finding faults, the more you will have thousands of reasons not to do it. You just need that indisputable attitude to get it done.

As I stood at the airport in my hometown, tears rolled down my cheeks as I bid goodbye to my family. In the four months that I had been in India following my dad's death, I had grown closer to my roots. My heart cried as I left my tiny city heading to fulfill my mission that was about to change the direction of my life once again.

When I returned to Dubai I was lost and refused to enter my house. We had left our house the way it was, and everything was in its place. Memories of my dad haunted me, and I somehow could not continue living there. The question was, "So where will I live then?" I needed a secure place to live and someone who I could call my own. I was lucky that I did not have to break my head on this as I met a loving family with whom I lived for about nine months. They ended up being close to me even after two decades.

You may be wondering why my mom did not accompany me? Looking back, the whole situation seemed uncanny since my dad was planning to relocate to India. As a first step toward implementing the plan, he had canceled my mom's visa, and even before we could put the rest of the plan in place my dad passed away and I was the only one left with the visa.

My plan was to close my dad's business and return home at the earliest. Like they say destiny had something else planned for me, and I one day received a call for an interview in a French bank. I was intrigued more than excited and wanted to experience the interview and ended up getting the job. I picked the phone and consulted my mom and finally ended up taking up the job. I had no clarity why I did this, but I knew somewhere deep inside that this is the right way forward. I knew I had nothing to lose as the worst case was to quit and go back. On my dad's business front, I negotiated a deal with the manager and exited the company.

This was the time when I also met my future husband, who was tall and handsome. They say marriages are made in heaven, but matches are surely done on earth. Ours was a marriage that was initiated at a time when my father was alive, although I was not aware of this at all. Since my dad was attending to his health, he had put this discussion on hold. I was barely 21 and Dad wanted me to get married; no wonder my husband still says that mine was a "child marriage" (pun intended!).

Mine was an era when girls would get married before they touched 25. If the girl ever had to remain unmarried until 25, then chances were that the girl would die unmarried; that's what we were made to believe by our parents. I still cannot comprehend why parents thought this way. While this is an entirely different topic of debate, let us continue with my journey for now.

Balancing the Wheel of Life
Eight months later my husband and I were married, and during our first anniversary our son was two months old. This was probably the fastest action I have taken in my life. No wonder everyone thinks my eldest son is my younger brother. Our initial marriage days were spent changing diapers and trying to figure out when we could get a decent nap between my son's activities. My husband's knowledge of child care needed a serious upgrade. When I was still at the hospital after my delivery, I had asked my husband to get a few things for the baby. He excitedly went to the supermarket and purchased items only to discover that he had purchased wet wipes instead of diapers. It was an entirely new world for both of us, and we were trying to get a foothold without the real guidance of elders.

We did not quite have a honeymoon nor did I experience a baby shower during my first pregnancy. I had given up a lot of these worldly pleasures willingly as I did not find it a big deal. Probably one of the reasons was that my husband did not really have a stable job at that time, as the economy was not at its best. His heart was always in setting up his own business, and my only dream was to support his dream. I continued working with the French bank and taking care of the family, allowing my husband to explore the business ground.

This was the time my husband, a civil engineer by profession, was contemplating a career into entrepreneurship. While I had a full-time job, he was not fully settled in his career. He, on the other hand, wanted to do something of his own as he could never see himself in a regular job. Without much planning, he ventured into working independently. This was the time when we were not even financially stable, but our spirits and attitude were in tandem.

His spirit was so high that he would wake up at 5:00 a.m. in the morning and set out to work. He had many roles to play and drove about 300–500 kilometers every day meeting clients and suppliers, and surveying the market. The intention to get things done was so deep-rooted that no rejections would disappoint him. All he wanted was to get his business take off the runway and fly high.

When you are passionate about your goal, your attitude aligns with your purpose. Check your passion levels often.

After persistent hard work, he managed to bag his first contract from a well-known client, a key foundation to our growth. At this time, my husband did not even have his own license but yet the client had faith in him and awarded him the job. With the same faith, this company remains to be our client even after two decades. This encouraged my husband to set up his first company in the year 1999. A much-needed identity was established with a small office. The following days were some of the best days of our life. While I was engaged in a full-time job, I would dedicate my evenings helping my husband to prepare quotes, track orders, and also discuss strategic matters. Together we had delivered our second child, that is, our own company that was dear to both of us.

In the next few years, we witnessed resounding success, and in the year 2005 we set up a new license with a limited liability status. This allowed us to take bigger jobs and claim more control over the company. The size of jobs we signed also grew with clients who were repeating their projects with us. With the many projects my husband executed, he built strong credibility in the market. His business ethics was based on the principle of giving more value to the client without compromising on quality. This made our clients happy, resulting in repeated business.

The initial days of struggle building up toward achieving our goals were like an acoustic rendition of a symphony whose visual glimpse was a far-sighted dream. Despite the shortage of resources, we were willing to put in our best efforts into making things work. During this time, we had less doubts and fear but more hope, drive, and passion to achieve our goals. We clearly knew at that stage that actions spoke louder than words. Without action, there is no progress and we were our own fortune cookies. We were baking our own cookies day and night, while investing a lot of hard work and making sacrifices equally.

But all I can remember is that this was the best phase of our life. There was no pressure to prove to anyone but to our inner self which was waiting to shout out to the world, The world is mine."

Path to Growth

I continued to grow on the professional front, learning new skills that I enjoyed. I had this undying passion within me that gave me the much-needed adrenaline to keep my spirits high even when the going got tough. I had still not ticked my bucket list of completing my degree, yet worked hard in whatever I did and continued to grow in different roles. In this path, I also learned new areas like financial analysis, credit risk, and corporate banking. I understood accounting and finance and everything else from scratch. With the help of my colleagues, I put the knowledge puzzle together step by step. I continued to ask questions and solved real-time problems, and in a matter of months, I was able to analyze the most complex of balance sheets and prepare multiple credit proposals.

I had picked up the ability to negotiate with clients and understand their business requirements by often accompanying the relationship managers during client visits. I became comfortable in meeting clients and understanding their trade, which helped me develop a mind attuned with business.

> *Make a conscious effort to associate with people or activities that will help you grow. They are your building blocks for a positive attitude.*

One of my "wow" moments as a financial analyst was when I was assigned the responsibility of renewing the credit facilities of a leading company. Since this was a well-established company, there was no reason to worry and at the face of it, the renewal was a cakewalk. When I deep-dived into the balance sheet and sought information, I picked certain crucial observations that were technically not the right way of reporting. I highlighted these to my credit manager while reassessing the file and proposed relevant conditions to secure the bank's interest.

This was one of the key highlights that saved a lot of headache for the bank, and one day the senior credit manager walked up to me and said, "You have a great future ahead."

This statement was an immune booster for me and revalidated my life mantra, "Be the best in whatever you do."

I continued to grow in the bank from one position to the other and finally got promoted as the Manager—Credit Control. This was quite an achievement from a junior to a manager of a world-class French bank in just eight years. It is not that I had anyone supporting me to rise to this position. In fact, it was a struggle for me at every point as I had people bringing up the reality of the missing degree. Although my burning desire to complete my education seemed unfulfilled, I was being appreciated for my efforts and meticulousness. I began to travel to foreign countries, with my first trip to Paris for a training at the headquarters of the French bank I worked with.

Sometimes you just need a few words of encouragement from others to renew your self-confidence. We all possess that achiever attitude in us, but sometimes our mind seeks validation from others to realize our self-worth. Being among supportive people helps here, and it is therefore important to consciously select the type of people you want to spend most of your time with. Those who can listen to you and appreciate your achievements will always help you in achieving your goals. This, however, may not always be possible, and therefore, loving yourself and being kind to yourself will help you a lot.

Together with my professional growth came my two other bundles of joys, another baby boy "Ashish," meaning blessing and a much-awaited girl child "Siya," which is the Sanskrit name for Goddess Sita. We were now proud parents of four kids, including our business, which was maintaining a linear equation with us. As I had planned, I had my three biological children before I hit 30 and also purchased our first apartment in Mangalore. This was the beginning of many such accomplishments that made our life sail smooth.

Ticket to Paris
My relationship with journey on flight began when I was 10 years old. Each year I would board the plane as an unaccompanied minor and land in Dubai for a month or two of royal treatment from my parents. I was not a stranger to traveling but, beyond my trips to Dubai, I had not seen any other place on the globe.

My new position as a credit control manager had opened doors for my travel to countries that I had not visited earlier. One such dream city was Paris, the fashion capital of the world, known for iconic structures like the Eiffel Tower, Champs Elysee, or even the Moulin Rouge. A place which is every traveler's dream and my dream came true in 2006 when I traveled for work to Paris.

"Bonjour Madam, Welcome to Air France," said a beautiful air hostess.

Quickly settling in my business-class seat, I eagerly looked forward to landing at the famous Charles De Gaulle airport. A week-long work assignment was waiting at the headquarters of my employer, an organization which gave me a strong reason to love Paris. But Paris was about to give me a reason to change the way I looked at life.

After a week, my son and my husband joined me for a holiday. One morning we purchased the train tickets to Disneyland, and my husband slipped the tickets in his shirt pocket. We arrived at the magical place of Disneyland where my favorite cartoon characters came alive. Minnie, Mickey, and Peter Pan showcased a rendezvous with my childhood. After an exciting morning, my son and I settled in a cozy corner of an open food court while my husband went to get food. As soon as he arrived, he asked for his wallet that he had given me before going to pick up the food.

> *Create a problem-solving attitude that will help you see possibilities more than challenges.*

I searched for it everywhere but could not find it. We had just been robbed of all our money. I felt helpless in a foreign country and had no money to get back to Paris. While I started getting dramatic, my husband was determined to get back to Paris and asked me not to dramatize the situation. He was determined and started searching his pockets. To our good luck, he pulled three tickets and 10 euros that he had slipped in his shirt pocket in the morning. We got back to Paris, and the first thing we did was pick up some cash from our hotel room locker and purchase a camera. What followed next was probably a failed holiday set right. That day I learned one important lesson: failures are bound to take place in life. But much of what follows after that depends on your attitude toward these failures.

When a large corporation fails it is the attitude of the leaders that matter. I had once read that Ford Motor was on the verge of bankruptcy in 2006. Its CEO Alan Mullaly turned around the company by not trimming ends but by creating value-based leadership through five bests: best self, best team, best partner, best investment, and best citizen. When we were robbed and left alone it was my husband's attitude that created value to our time spent in Paris. Instead of cutting our holiday, he turned around our experience by thinking out of the box. Right attitude helps you get through the highs and lows of life. If you have an attitude where you give up even before the event occurs, imagine what would be your state of mind when a crisis hits you.

Keys to Improving Your Attitude

1. Continue your passion even when the going gets tough. It helps develop an action-oriented attitude.
2. Don't let the entire staircase overwhelm you. Just focus on that first step.

3. When you are passionate about your goal, your attitude aligns with your purpose. Check your passion levels often.
4. Make a conscious effort to associate with people or activities that will help you grow. They are your building blocks toward positive attitude.
5. Create a problem-solving attitude that will help you see possibilities more than challenges—work on your behavior.

Your actions after reading this chapter
A conscious effort to work on your attitude will take you a long way, and the following are a few guidelines that you can consider implementing in your life:

1. Create a habit of affirmation by writing down your positive attitude.
2. Learn from every situation you face and find the gratitude quotient.
3. Consider setbacks as an opportunity to learn and grow.
4. Improve your patience level as it will help you improve your attitude.
5. Dedicate time for yourself.
6. Be kind on yourself and others—life is not a rule book but a book to set your own rules.

Chapter 7
Emotional Intelligence in Managing Stress

If you cannot manage stress, you will not manage success.

IN TODAY'S FAST-PACED world, chronic stress is becoming a part of people's lives, and human beings now accept that one cannot escape it if we continue to live the way we are. Stress is the result of the high-pressured life that the majority of the world is living. People's mind and body pay a high price for it. Stress is the result of your body not being able to cope up with the demands of an event. It can lead to various other problems if one ignores it for a long time. Stress is the first defense mechanism that the body uses. But not all stress is bad, and the hormones that the body produces in response to the stress aren't bad either. The levels of the hormones fluctuate throughout the day depending on the activity that you indulge in such as waking up (yes, that's an example of stress), dealing with office politics, or receiving a surprise gift.

Stress can help you in certain cases to stay alert and focused, like when you are holding a baby and it suddenly slips from your hand. Some perform well under stress and are also highly productive, like a student who has to submit an assignment within a set deadline. Stress at work can also produce good results as it sharpens your concentration, especially when you have to deliver that important presentation at work or have to study for an examination. But this is good only when it is within limits because after a certain point, stress stops being helpful and becomes the major cause of concern when the loss of appetite, loss of sleep, depression, and fatigue creep into your daily pattern of life. It also becomes a cause for personal problems, thus reducing the quality of life.

What Is Stress?
It is the body's natural defense against enemies and danger. The moment you are in stress is, therefore, dangerous as it causes the body to flood with hormones that prepare the system to confront or avoid danger. This is commonly referred to as a "fight-or-flight mechanism."

The body produces larger quantities of chemicals cortisol, epinephrine, and norepinephrine, which trigger physical reactions such as sweating, alertness, blood pressure, and stress on body muscles. The most common reasons for stress are said to be *employment* and *money*, and this was found through a survey conducted by the American Psychological Association (APA) in the year 2018.

Stress is another form of emotion that we all go through. For some people, a simple event could also lead to a situation of stress. As far as I can remember, I was not a person who would easily get stressed out with issues. I could also probably call myself ignorant or devoid of situations around me. This has a lot to do with the kind of serene childhood I had where neither my aunty nor my parents gave me any kind of stress. I had a normal childhood that was filled with great memories of pranks and fun. This was perhaps one of the key reasons why I had the mindset to face any challenge in life, be it facing my dad's death or even supporting my husband take that plunge into the entrepreneurial world.

But one realization that I had is that the past unattended emotional baggage can also be a major reason for stress. It is recommended that you settle old issues and not carry them forward with you for long. Stress builds up over a period of time without your knowledge. If left unchecked, severe stress—the kind that continues for months or years—is more apt to lead to serious illnesses than short-term stressors do.

You should be aware of the amount of trauma you put yourself through, as it finally shows up later in life when the stamina and strength to bear the stressful condition reduces with age. Probably this is what happened to me as well. I forgot that I have to be kind to myself, and there is a limit to what your body can endure. Beyond this even if you can sustain, all it means that you are running over capacity, and one day you are bound to break down.

This is where people also must learn to set boundaries in their actions. While you hear a lot of people talk about limitless growth and potential to break the ceiling, it is critical to understand your strength and weakness and your purpose in life, which will help you set some realistic goals.

Unexpected changes can also lead to a heightened feeling of stress as it pushes you out of your comfort zone. When this happens, it creates a feeling of uncertainty and loss of control leading to stress and anxiety. At this time, you probably must have heard many people tell you, "You can do it, everything will be fine, this too shall pass." What one needs to understand is that

Motivation alone doesn't work on externally imposed change—lead your way through it.

When stress breaks the ceiling of tolerance, clarity in mind reduces and the vision gets blurred. Your capacity to think clearly also reduces, not knowing how and when to eliminate unwanted emotions.

Stages of Change
But before that let us understand the stages one goes through when they face a change, which in this case is an unexpected change. Dr. Cynthia D. Scott and Dr. Dennis T. Jaffe developed the "Change Model" based on Dr. Elisabeth Kubler-Ross's, Kubler-Ross "Grief Curve." The change model explains that

a person going through change moves through these four stages: Denial, Resistance, Exploration, and Commitment.

I have used this model to indicate the role of emotional intelligence as a tool to understand and manage emotions and at what stage I applied this tool to manage the unexpected change.

THE CHANGE GRID

(Adapted from by Dr. Cynthia D. Scott and Dr. Dennis T. Jaffe's The Change Model)

EXTERNAL FOCUS

DENIAL	COMMITMENT
Procrastinate	Acceptance Progress Focus
Depression Sadness Anger	Opportunity Realization
RESISTANCE	**EXPLORATION**

Role of Emotional Intelligence

INTERNAL FOCUS

← PAST　　　　　FUTURE →

Everyone goes through this journey, but how fast you move through these changes depends on how you handle it. If you are going to consider unexpected change as negative then chances are you are going to remain in the first two quadrants of denial and resistance for a long time. This could lead to unwanted emotions like anger, depression, and argument.

If you make an effort to understand your emotions and manage them, then this will help you move to the quadrant of exploration and acceptance. This is what I experienced in my journey of unexpected change. The moment I stopped resisting change, I acquired the focus and clarity to move ahead in the direction of growth.

This was done by learning to be emotionally intelligent. People with high emotional intelligence are able to eliminate the unwanted emotion that does not serve their purpose. When you build the ability to use the right emotion at the right time, you thrive.

The following iceberg is a great example to illustrate the power of emotional intelligence. It is when you start understanding your emotions, managing them, and using them in the right way that you learn to see the huge benefits that lie deep within those challenges. Emotional intelligence helps you deep dive into the situation and explore a world of possibility that is not visible to naked eyes.

Once you develop your emotional intelligence, you also develop an ability to see through these challenges and start exploring the possibilities of opportunity leading to "acceptance and commitment."

This stage is most fulfilling as you realize that when you start lifting the self-imposed restrictions or limitations, you liberate yourself from a lot of negative aspects in your life. You are ready to let go off your past and start getting excited about your future.

Chapter 8
The Illusion Called Success

Success is not final, failure isn't fatal. It's the courage to continue that counts.

—*Winston Churchill*

I HAVE HEARD many of my friends complain that they are tired of their corporate jobs and wish to quit before hitting 50. A few even dreamed of setting up their own business and being their own boss. My reason for contemplating putting a break to my career was a bit personal.

"Ma'am, your son has to be more attentive in class, he speaks a lot," said one of the teachers during my older son Karthik's parent-teachers' meeting.

Each time I visited his school my urge to be a stay-at-home mom got stronger as I felt guilty about not being there for my son. The increased work pressure kept me away from home most of the time, and I felt I had worked far too long—having started work at the age of 17 as soon as I came to Dubai.

I sat down with my husband and spoke about me quitting my high-positioned job. My husband asked me to reconsider saying, "You should not look back and see it as a mistake, so please think carefully."

His concern was my individuality, as he always believed that it is important for a woman to have her own identity that primarily comes from her own achievement. At the same time, he did not force me to work as the business was doing well and he could easily take care of the family. But his opinion was inspired by the fact that his mom was a working woman and he has always seen her in a position of authority.

> *Keep unwanted emotions away when making crucial decisions in your life.*

My mother-in-law was a teacher who grew up to be a headmistress of a government school in his tiny village. She was one of the only two female students in the class who had enrolled for the teacher training course in the mid-1950s. She was well respected in the society and had thousands of students who adored her. My husband had grown up seeing a teacher in the house who was equally strict with her own children. For him, women were an epitome of strength and support and this is exactly what he saw in me too. As I had been his strength and backbone, he wanted me to make a career decision that would make me happy and not because of external factors.

Finally, I decided to take a break and submitted my resignation papers. This came as a rude shock to my manager and he was not happy with my decision. I was asked to reconsider my decision, and my request was pushed forward three times. I finally asked them to release me, and it was on July 8, 2008, after 11 long years of service with a bank, I embarked on yet another chapter in my life.

When I quit, I had a heartwarming farewell with the entire office showering me with gifts and messages. Although it was a goodbye hard to say, I was looking forward to my new life. I was 33 years old when I decided to quit my job and already had 17 years of experience behind me, but there was one unfulfilled dream that kept haunting me—my unfinished degree. I felt calm and was looking forward to spending time with my little kids who were elated with me around. It was those glorious days where I did not need anyone's permission to attend my son's parent-teachers' meeting. I was free to go for lunch with my husband, one of our favorite activities.

Journey from Manager to Director
Our company of eight years had grown significantly in size and credibility. We were financially capable, and I could take a break and attend to the kids who needed my attention. The first few months were pure bliss where I did not have to wake up to the sound of the alarm clock and dress up for work; instead, my routine included dropping my kids to the school bus and chatting with the other parents.

After a few days, my husband suggested that I allocate some of my time during the day to visit the office. I had no plans to start on another career journey so early in time. If this was the case then my offer at the bank was still open. But after four months I made a decision to visit our office to familiarize myself with the business and its operations. It was a completely different environment, unlike my corporate environment. It was face-to-face with ground reality and people with real struggles and success stories. It was an epiphany that corporate job came with the security of a world-class brand name, and conducting business was relatively much easier owing to the brand name. But being a business person was not that easy. I realized the struggles one goes through to build a business from scratch.

Although we had started this business together, my husband managed things on his own with his staff once the business had taken off. Although we intermittently discussed business sometimes, I was involved in my own career growth. Getting back to business, I now realized my husband had come a long way. When I came in tune with reality, I was so proud of him with the way he had managed to build the business on his own.

Slowly and steadily I got involved in the financial management of the business. From one-bedroom office space, we moved to a bigger officer in a matter of two years. Once again, my husband found great support in me as I was instrumental in regularizing the internal controls of the company. Even before we could realize it we had another tag attached to our relationship; from life partners, we were now business partners too.

> *Success must not be at the cost of personal life. A healthy balance between family and business is imperative.*

Slowly and steadily we started executing multi million-dollar contracts with impressive client profiles. We had well-experienced people joining us to help us grow the business, and I had pretty much reached a comfort level that I was not too comfortable with. My burning desire to complete my education was still haunting me day and night, and internally there seemed to be an urge to explore more than what I had seen. To start with, the comfort level was eating my creativity; and I wanted to expand my wings beyond what I was currently doing, initially by making more friends.

A life without clear purpose is a recipe for distraction, and one starts losing interest with what you are doing. Purpose is required to bring clarity to mind and to keep you motivated toward achieving your goals. Although we worked tirelessly toward achieving success, somewhere our purpose was not very clear. We often asked ourselves, "Is this what life is all about? Constantly in a race for accomplishing?" We never had an answer to this, as a result of which our life was filled with a greater amount of business-related matters and lesser amount of other matters that had once involved us. Although we had a pact that no business would be discussed once we get home, the growing pressure and lack of clarity naturally pushed us to discussing business. This added a lot of pressure in our lives, but somewhere we managed to find a balance by deliberately ignoring certain matters.

We were still not well experienced in balancing life. Considering my meticulous nature, I had the tendency to take things seriously. This meant too much time given to discussing the pros and cons of the matter and eventually allowing it to dominate the conversation at home. I was impatient and temperamental too, which made it all the more difficult to balance the personal and professional life. Thanks to my husband, I managed to keep my anger under check over all these years. He was the best anchor in my life who would remain calm even in the most difficult situation. We were poles apart in personality, but like the saying "opposite poles attract," we were each other's anchors. I had a fierce go-getter attitude and would constantly boost his morale, and he was the calm and rational type who would keep me grounded.

Student Forever
While I was trying to do something different in my life, I wanted to begin with making new friends. In December 2013, I attended an international public speaking and leadership platform. The purpose of visiting this club was only one—make new friends. The day I visited as a guest, I was given a table topic and also awarded the best speaker award. This definitely made me feel special, and I signed up for the membership with the club. Unknowingly this became the start of an entirely new journey and a beginning to many more discoveries of my hidden talent and personality.

I thought I was a confident speaker, owing to my convent education and confidence. But it is when I spoke in front of the audience in the club, I understood that public speaking is a skill to be gradually learned with patience and practice. It is only later that I learned that communication is the most powerful tool for growth. It has the power to set you on the pedestal of success when you learn to communicate the right way at the right time.

I have always given preference to continuous learning, and it is one aspect that still has high relevance in my life. If it was not for continuous education, I would have probably not made so much progress in life. I had not given up my dream of completing my education, and in the year 2017, I completed my MBA with Manchester Business School, UK, with a merit that was the icing on the cake.

> *Continuous learning is the only tool that will keep you grounded. Be a life long learner.*

Apart from my academic achievements, I also progressed in the communication and leadership domain. Along the way, I met a few wonderful mentors who guided me to take the right turns in my path and take up challenges. One such challenge was when my mentor asked me to take up the role of a "Mystery Speaker" for a contest without telling me what it was all about. When I arrived at the venue, I saw about 400 people sitting in the auditorium, taking me by surprise. This was the first time I was addressing such a huge audience, delivering a solo speech. Instead of getting cold feet I took a deep breath and delivered my speech for which I received a huge applause. Even before I realized, the doors of an entirely new world had opened for me and I discovered a new person in me.

I developed a passion for speaking and also realized my ability to connect with people through speech. This was validated by the fact that I was able to negotiate better deals with banks at work and also build relations, which was initially a bit difficult for me. I always thought about myself as an introvert when it came to making friends, but here I also learned the real meaning of introvert. Although I liked my loneliness, I enjoyed being among people who were friendly, warm, and helped each other grow. I never knew that this world even had people who genuinely wanted others to succeed in life—they are called "mentors."

This time I was introduced to this new concept called mentors, who would listen to you, guide you, and also correct you. It was a "wow" moment for me and I felt that if each one did this for other's growth, how beautiful the world would be. Although the term mentor was new to me, looking back I always had a mentor in my life, be it my grandmother, my dad, or my colleagues in the office. They were the guiding force in building my confidence and personality. But this time this was done in a way I was completely aware of the benefits, and I was also in a position to make good use of their selfless service.

This is when I was also introduced to the concept of "Relationship Management" and learned that there is no life without people, and relationship is the basis for human growth. It is through people that we grow, and it is through growth that we seek to create an impact in this world. Growth is meaningless if you have not understood yourself well since it is only when you understand yourself well are you able to connect with people with authenticity. This was the key to building authentic relationships with people: "self-awareness."

Putting people first teaches the value of human existence.

I slowly began to discover the person in me, my strengths, and my dreams. Until now I had gone with the flow like a fierce bull. I was running in a direction that did not seem to be there in reality. I was doing what the world wanted me to do, be it my corporate job, our business, or anything else I did in my life. Now I began to understand that while it is important to go with the flow, it is also important to do what you feel you are meant to do. This, you learn after several attempts of understanding yourself. I felt somewhere I had begun discovering the person in me.

This discovery had nothing to do with career or materialistic accomplishments, but it was more about discovering me and the world around me. I started accepting people the way they are and not judging them. This helped me build relationships with others, and the ego of "I" was slowly taken over by the magical word "We." This was a different kind of success that had nothing to do with materialistic satisfaction. In all probability, I was moving up the Maslow's Pyramid of Hierarchy. My purpose was being redefined and I was enjoying it. It seemed like my purpose was getting clearer by the day and what started bringing me joy was much more than what I had assumed was the concept of success.

What Is Your Purpose?
I was barely six months old in my public speaking journey, when I was asked to join the executive committee of the club, which I gladly accepted. The following year the mentor of the club walked up to me asking me to take up the role of the president. Initially, I resisted a lot as I had just enrolled for my MBA and had a business to take care of. He did not accept a "no" for an answer, and I ended taking up the role. To conduct my role effectively, he left me with a piece of profound advice:

"As a leader if you are ever confused about the right decision to make, always stand by the decision that will benefit your members."

Through his advice, he communicated the importance of "knowing your purpose." Isn't this true in real life too? Many times, we set out to achieve our dreams assuming it will make us happy, soon to realize that we are on the road of an endless battle of "wants," losing our core purpose. This is the illusion called success which looks like success, but when you get closer to it you realize that more needs to be done. Even in leadership one goes through the same dilemma. We start off with a lot of enthusiasm and bagfull of values, but when personal motives take over the purpose, leadership becomes a difficult task.

> **When you align your actions with your purpose, you will know that setbacks are only temporary.**

It is an illusion to think that success will fetch us happiness. Till the time we are unable to define the meaning of happiness, success is just a hide-and-seek game. It pays to have goals in life, but a goal without purpose is like a heart without soul. Something like this happened to my husband and me too. We had achieved what we had set out to achieve, but along the way, we failed to anchor our lives with a purpose. To do this you have to pause and listen to your own emotions, know your values, and know how your strength and weakness can support or limit you in your journey.

The Lost Wallet

One October afternoon my husband and I together with our kids were invited to our neighbor's birthday party. We all dressed up and embarked on a drive to the venue; on the way I was trying to finish a few pending tasks while my husband was driving. The first task was to book a flight ticket for my husband who was to travel the next day. Since things have become relatively convenient, I booked the ticket online using my smartphone. As I reached the payment page, I took my husband's card for the payment. I was so glad everything went well and finally I had a confirmation number on hand.

After the party, we started our journey back home, talking about the party we just attended. As we reached home my husband asked to disembark while he went and parked the car.

But before that, he said, "Give me my wallet."

"Which wallet?" I asked.

"The wallet that I had given you earlier to make the payment."

I realized that I had totally forgotten to return the wallet to him while getting down from the car. I backtracked our journey and remembered that I had kept the wallet on my lap and perhaps dropped it as I got down from the car. The wallet contained cash, debit card, driving license, identity card, insurance card—all in one single place.

I was extremely angry at my carelessness as history had repeated, the first time being in Paris. My husband and I immediately rushed back to the venue to the place where we had parked the car. We frantically searched the parking area while requesting the security to replay the security TV. To our utter dismay, the recording did not capture the area our car was parked. After spending several hours in that basement working out the permutation and combination, we returned home disappointed. While arguing and discussing the probabilities of the "ifs" and "buts" we only hoped that a miracle would take place.

At 6:00 p.m. in the evening my husband's mobile rang from an anonymous number. As he received the call a man on the other side said, "This is the police officer speaking. A man walked into our station just now and handed over your wallet and we found your contact number. If it is your wallet can you come over right now and collect it."

We just could not believe our ears as it felt like a symphony playing the Beethoven notes that elevated our mood. My husband and older son Karthik rushed to the police station to receive the precious wallet that was about to save us from several days of unwanted trips to the government departments. As my husband received the wallet, he noticed something was wrong. While some portion of the money was obviously missing, some of the cards were also not inside the wallet. The wallet certainly did not seem to be in its original state. Thank God we had already called the bank and blocked our cards.

The police mentioned that someone found it on the main road and handed it over to the police. My husband did not delve much into the nuances of the matter and did what was required at that moment. He was certainly relaxed after a long anxious day and came home to narrate the incident to me. That night when I went to bed a thought came to my mind, which was yet another eye-opener for me.

In life, we often take our relationships for granted, assuming that they will be with us forever, no matter what. But just like the wallet that slipped off my lap we never realize that our precious relationships could also one day slip off from our life, should we fail to take care of them. If we are lucky and if it does return to us, then it might not come back into our lives in its original form, just like the wallet. This realization also drew my attention to how important it is to take care of my relationships. I was often guilty of not giving enough time to my loved ones, being engrossed in my daily activities.

> **Success without people is a heart without soul.**

We run behind things thinking it would give us success and satisfaction but only to realize that there is nothing called as success in life. Success is a journey and not a destination. Anything that makes you feel complete and happy could be your meaning of your success. Unfortunately, human beings have associated the meaning of success with fame, money, and material gains. Once all of this is achieved, we ask ourselves, what next?

Then how could this be the meaning of success? Success is just an illusion. True meaning of success for me is the effort I put to bounce back in spite of my failures, the mistakes that I make and see the learning in them, the excitement I feel when I get the Best Speaker award, the feeling of pride when my child gets that Individual Cup in sports, and numerous other little things that make me smile.

Keys to Understanding the Meaning of Successful Life

1. Keep unwanted emotions away when making crucial decisions in your life—it could potentially distort the meaning of Success.
2. Success must not be at the cost of personal life. A healthy balance between family and business is imperative.
3. Continuous learning is the only tool that will keep you grounded. Be a lifelong learner—Success is the wisdom to find simplicity in every complex situation.
4. Putting people first teaches the value of human existence—your core to a successful life.
5. When you align your actions with your purpose, you will realize that setbacks are only temporary.
6. Success without people is a heart without soul.

Your actions after reading this chapter

1. Take time to list down your priorities in life and the time you are giving them.
2. Match your actions to your purpose in life—do they reconcile?
3. Take a reality check of whether your life is fully dependent on external circumstances for happiness.
4. Check your emotional quotient by taking an EQ or EI test online if you have not taken it earlier.

Chapter 9
Emotional Intelligence and Empathy

Empathy works so well because it does not require a solution. It requires only understanding.

—John Medina

ONCE WHEN I was in primary school, I had got very low marks in a subject. My parents were on a holiday visiting me at that time, and I was nervous to take the result home. Since my dad was there, I was confident that he would save me from my mom's wrath. I gathered my courage and went up to my parents and told them the truth. To my surprise, my mom said, "It is okay, you can try next time. I know the efforts that you have put in." These words gave me a renewed energy and confidence to trust my parents when things went wrong. This is what empathy does to a human being.

Empathy is the ability to understand the feelings of others by putting yourself in their shoes in a meaningful way. This is a powerful way in which you can not only touch lives but also make this world a better place to live. Being empathetic to someone's situation and feeling not only gives you a better understanding of their suffering but also helps you to build meaningful relationships. Imagine when you are available to listen to a friend who is going through a trauma in their life. All they need is a patient ear whom they can trust. Your friend will start talking to you in open and also trust you. This leads to better communication in relationships and also builds long-term friendships.

> *We must learn to regard people less in the light of what they do or omit to do, and more in the light of what they suffer.*
>
> —*Dietrich Bonhoeffer*

This does not mean that you have to share these emotions with them, but develop an understanding of what they are going through so you can respond appropriately to a situation. Empathy is an emotional intelligence competency and falls under social awareness.

Why Is Empathy Important?
Absence of empathy defeats the very core of human existence. Without consideration for others, you limit your perspective of the world. It is very easy to pass judgments on others without understanding their journey. This could lead to misunderstanding, low self-esteem, stressed relationship, or even loss of trust. Employees feel like a part of the organization when

they are heard and they feel valued. This results in better morale and productivity, which in turn helps the organization.

Leaders like Nelson Mandela and Mahatma Gandhi were successful because they not only had a vision, but their vision reverberated with the sentiments of people. The people felt that their leader cared for them and they could trust them easily.

What Stops Us from Being Empathetic?
There are several reasons that stop people from being empathetic. But what stands out for me are the following reasons:

1. **Insecurity**: This category of people does not necessarily feel insecure about someone threatening their job or growth. It has more to do with their own personal insecurities and the inability to balance their emotions. I have personally met people who are not empathetic because they are insecure with their own emotions. It has nothing to do with you, but it is their own internal struggles that they go through. One major factor is when they set high standards from themselves and are in constant pressure to perform. At this stage, they ignore all the people around them and are not even empathetic toward their own loved ones. They do realize their shortcoming but are unable to do anything about it. Once the task on hand is complete, they realize that they now need to pay some attention to you. Obviously, there are people who deliberately do not like to be empathetic as they feel threatened by others.
2. **Take people for granted:** This is another category of people who believe that they are entitled to every generosity from others but do not believe in reciprocating.

They create a perception about others in their mind and structure their behavior accordingly. They easily categorize people according to their social, physical, or economic status and show empathy only with expectation in return. When we are judgmental about people, we lose our ability to be empathetic toward them.

Again, these are all emotions that work in our mind, which are also associated with a feeling of fear. The basis for all behavior and attitude is our emotion, and empathy is a result of our attitude that we develop toward people and the world. The more strained our mind is, the more we diminish our capacity to think about others and their worries. It is thus all about us, resulting in our inability to build genuine relationships with others. This naturally reflects in the work we do as authenticity cannot be camouflaged with words or actions. It will be evident to others within no time.

How to Be More Empathetic?

To be empathetic, you have to first work on being emotionally intelligent by understanding not only your emotions but also that of others. This comes with conscious practice of the following:

1. **Being authentic helps:** Anything that comes straight from your heart connects with people. When you share your concern or stories from your heart without a mask it makes you real. Also being real with your own feelings helps you to accept your situation and acknowledge your feelings. This is the best way to liberate yourself from negativity and move ahead. When you are able to understand the deeper issues of

the situation you will be able to be empathetic toward yourself and the other person and will understand the situation better.
2. **Imagine what others are going through:** Try to understand why others are behaving the way they are and what could possibly be the reason for their behavior. It does not mean that you always have to find reasons to justify others' behavior, but avoid jumping to conclusions without understanding their side of the story. There is always a reason why one behaves the way they do, and when you understand this, it becomes easy to be compassionate and empathetic.
3. **Tell others and yourself often, "It's okay":** Setting high standards for yourself is one of the main reasons why you fail to understand others. You become so harsh on yourself that the unreasonable standards create a myopic view about the world. Sustainable performance comes with better conditions, and therefore allow yourself to make mistakes and avoid taking your failure as a big mistake. It is only through mistakes that you learn to set things straight. Excuse yourself and others for mistakes; after all, you are dealing with human beings. Say "It's okay" often, and when you accept yourself and the people the way they are you allow yourself to be more tolerant and empathetic.

The highest form of knowledge is empathy.

—*Bill Bullard*

Chapter 10
The Divine Storm

Nothing is more important than empathy for another human being's suffering. Nothing—not career, not wealth, not intelligence, certainly not status. We have to feel for another if we're going to survive with dignity.

—Audrey Hepburn

THEY SAY WHEN a loved one leaves to eternity without a closure, the soul wanders around. It is all good in books and videos, but when it happens in real it can chill you to the bone. My dad left this world without seeing my mom and me, and what I experienced next revalidated the bond we shared with each other.

The afternoon after my dad's funeral, my mom and I slept for a while as we were very tired. As soon as I fell asleep, in my dream, I saw a hand stretching toward me asking for my hand.

I could then feel my hand stretching out, but even before holding that hand, I woke up. It seemed very strange and was not sure what had just happened, but it all felt very real. I narrated this to my mom who said, "It will take a while for your mind and heart to accept that dad is no more. Your mind is just trying to create situations to make you believe that he is around."

The next day again when I was asleep another message was waiting to be delivered in my dreams. Drinking water in some Indian homes is stored in traditional clay dispenser to keep it cool and fresh, and we had this system in our house too. All of a sudden, I saw this dispenser moving and it was like someone was asking me for some water. Once again, I blamed my psyche that was trying to create events in my dad's memory.

The final nail in the coffin was the third day, when we were still in deep grief and mourning. That night when I fell asleep, history repeated—my dad's mortal remains were placed in our hall, and as I entered, I saw my dad opening his eyes and telling me, "I was waiting for you, my love, give me some water."

As I poured water in his mouth it seemed like I had just calmed the unsettling waves in the ocean. My dad was finally happy and relieved that he had seen his beloved daughter and wife and it was now time for him to leave forever. From that day onward I never had a single dream of my dad asking for anything. This was one of the unforgettable experiences that I had after my dad's death. But for me, these were divine signs

> *A proper closure helps you make better decisions and move on in life.*

that my dad was finally happy to "Rest in Peace." After this incident, my relatives told me that before dad passed away, he was crying to see me and mentioned he would not leave without that.

Emotional Baggage
I was now on a struggle between the mind and heart being constantly reminded of my core purpose in life. My heart was regurgitating the sentiment that it was now time to do something I always wanted to do. My passion seemed to be gradually sprouting from the bud of skepticism that made it harder. It was already 15 years to our marriage, and I had matured as a woman from the little girl I was. My dad's trauma lived with me for a long time but somehow after the birth of my children, it seemed to have settled down. My busy life did not give me time to think about the emotions that I thought I had left behind. Days passed, but what became more and more evident was that my emotions wanted to talk to me. All these years, they felt deprived of my attention and now they would burst out even at the silliest of instance.

In 2016, my older son Karthik got admission in the United States to pursue his undergraduate degree. He was my strength and anchor in life. We literally grew up together as I was only 22 years old when I had him. I cannot claim I was the best mother because he had to bear the brunt of my trial-and-error parenting. We are close buddies, and he grew up listening to all my stories and the countless talks we had during our road trips. Perhaps this is the reason why he was inclined to take up law as he knew this was my dream too. But I had not forced any profession on him, and what he chose was purely a result of his aspiration. We traveled to the United States as a family to drop him at the university.

The United States, a dream for many, felt like magic for me, and I was landing in a place that I had always heard stories about. It felt good to experience another dream come true, and my son was excited as he was about to experience a new life. We started off with a 10-day leisure tour of the east side of the United States and finally reached our destination, the Indiana University in Bloomington. The sprawling campus at the university was any student's dream. We reached the dorm and helped Karthik settle into his new home for the next four years. After 20 days of our stay in the United States, we bid goodbye to our first born with a heavy heart and returned to Dubai.

Days passed with the void growing bigger and bigger in my heart. I felt that my arms were pulled apart by an unknown force and my anchor in life was not with me anymore. I always thought of myself as a practical and unemotional parent who would not cling to her kids. But to my surprise, the next six months were too hard on me. The feeling of being lost took a toll on me and I found it difficult to gather my spirits together.

My two other children were on their own journey of learning and living and did not depend much on my physical support, unlike how attached I was to Karthik. This made me lonely, and how much ever I tried, it was hard to make things go back to normal. I often discussed this with my husband who tried to console me with rationality, but it seldom worked for me. For the next one year, I suppressed my emotions and kept myself busy in completing my MBA and felt everything was back to normal. But when I finished my MBA the void came back with double the force. This time I faced tremendous mood swings with my dad's memories. Each moment I sat idle or the emotional moments in any movie made me cry out loud.

"You were never like this before," I told myself.

I tried to control my emotions, but the more I tried, the more my dad's abrupt departure resurfaced. I tried keeping myself busy by pursuing my passion and my attention toward my business was affected. Emotionally I was growing weaker and did not find enough strength to make firm decisions. This was not like me, as I was focused with a lot of clarity in my mind. I never thought that buried emotions would be a reason for my trouble in life. I kept complaining about how unfair it was for my mom to keep me away from her.

I must confess that I have not been the greatest of daughter to my mother. Owing to my distance from childhood I easily got into arguments with her. All the emotional baggage made matters worse, and even before I realized the carpet under my feet was swept off. It was a sort of disorientation of life and I had lost it. I felt my life was spiraling downward so badly that it was hard to remain strong.

Emotional baggage from the past plays a crucial role in our present state of mind. If we do not have a proper closure then it is difficult to remain balanced, and these emotions will keep showing up. If you want to move ahead in life, first settle your scores with your past, and only then you can move forward to embrace the world of opportunity that lies ahead of you. This also applies to relationships that carry some traumatic memories that continue to affect you. You must try to settle the matter with those people before you can move ahead in life.

Aim to keep your emotions as light as possible as toxic emotions must be avoided in all your thinking. It does not serve your purpose nor does any good to others. It only eats up your good self like a termite that weakens the furniture in your house.

Edge of the Cliff
My mood variation was something that I kept to myself and never spoke about it. But when it started recurring quite often, I decided to have a discussion with my husband. Initially, he did not take it seriously but slowly realized that I needed help. We were not in our best of form although our understanding with each other was so strong that we wanted to sail through this. We knew we were heading to some testing times and that it could potentially turn our life upside down. I kept myself busy with my passion for public speaking and managed to deliver speeches even when I was not in my best of forms.

This, until now, seems to be a miracle to me. I managed to switch moods when I was in a passion zone that I loved. My husband appreciated that I did my best to keep moving ahead despite my not-so-great health condition. He always complained that I spent too much time there and that I was not taking care of myself. When I started facing emotional highs and lows, the possibility of health complication seemed inevitable, and he felt helpless. I surely needed to put in a big effort to pull myself out of the chaos that was happening inside me.

One day I woke up in the morning holding my head on either side with both my hands. I looked at the ceiling lying on my bed with my head spinning like a fan on high speed. I could not stop it and did not know what was going on. I just wanted someone to switch off the button inside my head to stop it from spinning. I just closed my eyes and waited for the momentum to reduce, and when it did, I slowly turned to my right. It started spinning again and all I could do was continue lying on the bed.

> **Understand that you do not have solutions to all your problems.**

After some time, I woke up and narrated the incident to my husband. It was the first time I was going through something like this and had no idea what this was. I kept facing this intermittently, and it began to bother me. I had read about vertigo, but I had never before gone through this problem in my life. I googled to find more information and found out that this happens when there is an infection in the ear, but I had none. What else could it be? I did get headaches often, but this couldn't be the reason why my head was spinning. It was also accompanied by continuous moments of despair where I felt tired, low, and nervous.

My husband and I visited our family doctor who chose to underplay it and asked me to rest well; he has known us for more than 20 years, and we are like family. My life was at its lowest point, and all I was seeking was self-pity and sympathy from others. I could not stand up for myself nor make any decision but only complain about how things have been unfair to me. The only silver lining that I had was my ability to speak out loud. Being the vocal person I was, I did not hesitate to reach out and speak.

The blessing is that I have a husband who is willing to listen like a friend. If we went through a rough day he would understand and we would seek solutions rather than blame each other. One day I made him and a long-time friend sit in front of me and discussed all the internal troubles that I was facing. My husband and my friend were well aware of my childhood trauma of living away from my parents and losing my dad too early in life. My husband was so understanding that he said, "Why don't you discuss the issues with your friend more in open, if that helps you?"

I could never think of a man so understanding who at my worst emotional low felt that all options have to be explored to make me feel better. Little did he know that I could never feel comfortable with anyone but him as he was my boxing pad!

My husband has been practicing yoga for several years now, and till today he has a personal trainer who visits our house daily to train him. This is the age-reversal yoga technique that he began due to his back problem. This yoga instructor was also a therapist who would deal with both body and mind.

> **You need an empathetic ear and not always an advice to help you deal with the storm—listen more.**

To provide me more help one day my husband fixed a session with the instructor without my knowledge. As the instructor entered my house, he started to inquire about me. Initially, I was surprised why he chose to ask my well-being, but I continued to talk to him without hesitation. That session helped me a lot to talk about my state of mind. He patiently listened to me, and that day I felt good about talking to someone who was willing to listen and not advise.

I learned during this time that a person going through a storm inside needs an empathetic ear and not a box of advice. Everyone knows what to do, but lack of clarity due to stress is what blurs the vision. Clarity is achieved when the emotional baggage is offloaded from the heart and mind, which is possible by talking it out and discussing it in a manner that leads to a forward-looking mindset. Divine storms are not those that come to destroy you but to teach you a lesson. In my case, I had the emotional baggage that I carried with me for very long which was not attended to properly. I was too busy with achieving my professional aspiration, while the internal conflicts began to rise. The good thing was that I became aware of this and started thinking in a manner which helped me create awareness of my emotion. Unknowingly, I was being emotionally intelligent and this was helping me out, although I had a long journey ahead. This was also the reason why I was finding it difficult to deal with my mother, which had internally affected our relationship in my mind.

Blessing in Disguise
Unexpected changes take place in life without a warning, but signs in my life were quite evident, although the outcome was a

total surprise. It felt like the divine change was happening behind the scene, and all plans were underway to put me on a path that would serve my renewed purpose in life. The problem was my purpose was still not clear to me, but I knew it was all meant to change. Change for the better with turbulence that would seem quite disturbing. But I had no clue what was going to happen next and I was just doing what I was meant to do now. Some of my actions were still impulsive; as they say, "Old habits die hard." But the situation was such that impulsiveness was the only way out. Sometimes when we mull too much over things, we see logic in a manner that stops us from taking action.

> *It is okay to feel the way you are feeling. Forgive yourself and others often and you will begin empathizing more.*

Although my purpose was not clear, at least I realized that the purpose was important. Finding purpose is a journey in itself. It is not something that you wake up one morning shouting "Eureka, eureka." It is a result of who you are as a person and what motivates you to move ahead. I was not in a hurry to find my purpose because I knew that with time, I will realize it, provided I kept putting in sincere efforts to find it. But before I could find it, I had to first find myself.

Purpose and passion are two sides of the same coin, and it is passion that ignites the purpose in life. But the crossroad I had faced did not allow me to see the philosophical side of things. All I wanted was to escape from the situation and put myself in a spot where no one but I alone existed. I needed to make friends with myself, heal myself, and attend to the internal discord that was long overdue. From a person who had all the strength to handle the toughest of situations, to a person who would cry at the drop of a hat, my resilience had taken a steep dive.

It is a known fact that human beings resist change. We have all heard from time immemorial that it is because of "fear of unknown." But it is because of what we think we know about the unknown that human beings resist change. If it was left to me, I was too comfortable with my life, and though I felt the need for the drastic change, things would have still remained unchanged for a very long time. But over the years I had made way for a lot of unwanted stress in my life, both internally and externally, and this is where I felt the universe was conspiring to make the change for me. Change was inevitable, and I had no control over it. When I look back it was a divine storm that seemed ferocious from the outside, but inside me, it helped to transform me as a person.

What was waiting next was about to change my direction of life once again and this time for even better.

Keys to Understanding Empathy

1. A proper closure helps you to take better decisions and move on in life.
2. Understand that you do not have solutions to all your problems.
3. You need an empathetic ear and not always an advice to help you deal with the storm—listen more.
4. It is okay to feel the way you are feeling. Forgive yourself and others often, and you will begin empathizing more.

Your actions after reading this chapter

1. Take some time to think if there is anything that is bothering you.
2. Are you repeatedly allowing this to bother you?
3. If you do not want to discuss this then write down your feelings. Crush this paper and throw it away when you are done. Repeat this for at least a week and see if you are feeling better.
4. If not, record your feelings on your phone, listen to it, and delete it after three days.
5. Relax your body and mind by releasing the stressful thoughts through this procedure.
6. Meditate for at least 15 minutes per day and make this your routine.

Chapter 11
Managing Unexpected Change

The art of life lies in a constant readjustment to our surroundings.

—*Kakuzo Okakura, The Book of Tea*

EMOTIONAL INTELLIGENCE IS a powerful tool that helps you manifest your thoughts into reality by understanding and managing your emotions efficiently. We can argue incessantly about how success is achieved. It was Winston Churchill who once said, "Success is walking from failure to failure with no loss of enthusiasm." It is up to you to decide which way you will opt to pull yourself through your failures. For me, the best way has been starting it right from me.

If you have faced an unexpected change in your life and you are waiting for the right time and the right person to rescue you, let me remind you that "20% don't care and the other 80% are glad you have them." This quote has always left an impact in my mind, not because of the sarcasm it entails but due to the stark reality of life. No one is going to rescue you when you face an unexpected change. If you have one or two friends to show you empathy, please consider yourself lucky.

Unexpected situations do not pick and choose people, and the rule of the game is the same for everyone. Look at the COVID-19 situation; no borders, barriers, or social status of people stopped this virus from spreading across the continents. Same is the case with what happens in life. While you cannot escape from reality, the only arm that you can adorn is your *Resilience* to deal with it. I did this by being emotionally intelligent because before I set out to put things straight, I had to clear the confusion inside me. I cannot claim that I have done it all by now, because it is a journey. What is important is that I am seeing significant progress, and I am able to manifest a lot of things into the direction I want to take them.

So, what can you do once you have shown some progress in the area of being emotionally intelligent? Being emotionally intelligent is one thing and the ability to set things straight is another. Because even after being emotionally intelligent if you are not systematic in manifesting the change, then the results may not be as per your heart's desire.

This is where a structured approach and greater awareness of how to deal with the process comes to your rescue. While chances are that you will be overwhelmed with certain unexpected changes, the first step is to understand your emotions and learn how to manage them. Although this is an internal matter, the externally imposed change can be managed by being aware of what comes next.

Five Steps to Dealing with Unexpected Change

STEP 1: Accept Change
The first way to ease the stress is to accept what is going on in your life. Living in denial will only make matters worse. Accept the reality of the moment and tell yourself that it is something that will bring a different dimension to life.

STEP 2: Acknowledge Your Feelings
Without acknowledging your emotions, you are being harsh on yourself. You are expecting the wound will heal while picking on it every day. In order to move forward, it is extremely crucial to allow yourself to experience and go through the

emotions you are feeling, whether positive or negative. These experiences teach you a lot of lessons and help you shed your emotional baggage, making it easier to embrace the future. It will help you move through the pain and not with the pain. Stop blaming others and take ownership of your situation because accountability gives direction.

STEP 3: Explore Your Options
Mind is a complex matter, and the reason why it fears change is because of the "out of balance"/"out of control" feeling. Mind has an uncanny quest to feel in control, so when you face unexpected change it is important to find out what is still under control. Find out what is good for you in this change. Asking empowering questions will help you adopt a progressive mentality. It will help you understand that change is inevitable and is part of the process. When you start seeing value in the change, you will not feel like a victim of the situation.

STEP 4: Respond Appropriately—Stay Motivated
Patience is a virtue; avoid being dramatic about the change. A clear mind and perspective can help you respond rather than react that you may regret later. Take a walk and have a pet at home that will help you to cope up with the change. The impact of the unexpected change also depends a lot on how you respond to the situation. If you consider it as negative then everything will seem like a burden to you, but if you choose to see the brighter side, you will see hope and happiness.

STEP 5: Reach Out for Guidance: Keep Networking Alive
When in doubt ask for help. It is the strongest of people who reach out for help when required. This is the time when you

consciously need to maintain your network of people you know and develop it further. This may not be possible initially, but after you have given yourself some time to sink into the situation, you can consciously make an effort to build your network and contacts.

But let me remind you that managing change with a clear direction makes the journey enriching. Therefore, the following aspects will have to be considered before you set out on your journey of managing unexpected change.

- Dig Deep
- Recreate Life's Purpose
- Be Open to Possibilities
- Do not Resist

Chapter 12
The Road to Self-Discovery

It's your road, and yours alone. Others may walk it with you, but no one will walk it for you.

—*Rumi*

IMAGINE YOU HAVE gone on a foreign trip and during your sightseeing tour you end up in a place that was not in your itinerary. You initially get irritated with the guide for this confusion and are forced to tour the place. Unwillingly, you start exploring and soon realize this place is a hidden gem. You wonder how you could have missed this place in your plan, and thank the guide for the error. This is what happens when you are on a road to discovery. In my case, it was my life journey that I was discovering, but the sentiments that I echoed were similar to the above.

In the year 2019, I visited India on a holiday with my two kids. This journey was unlike my previous holidays that I had. It seemed like I was on a mission that was not clear to me. I decided to move to India two years later owing to my kid's college education. But this one had come earlier than I had planned. All the signs from the universe were pointing toward the inward journey that was long overdue. I had to tally the balance sheet of life that was totally out of balance at this point. All I wanted to do was listen to my heart and do what was needed. It was time I released the old baggage so I was fit to make peace with my present life. There was already too much that I was doing that was not giving me enough time to deal with my internal disharmony. I finally took the call to leave everything behind and move to India at least for some time.

The journey begins with accepting change— experience it to grow in abundance.

Similar to my previous impulsive moves, I decided to apply the brake to my life that seemed to have emotionally spiraled down. I finally decided to walk on that long journey I was not sure when it would end. All I knew was that I wanted to walk this journey as long as I could find peace with myself. I must admit that I did not have clarity of what is going to happen in the future but all I did was what I felt was required at that time. Like always, I knew that I would find my way, and this time it was definitely the hard way. I had stripped myself of my identity as I had left everything behind and decided to reboot my life. I must admit that this must have been the epitome of audacity in my life.

I had to walk back 27 years to experience a union of sorts. Everything seemed new to me as I could not recognize my own tribe, my own city, and the smell of the soil that once gave me the reason to come back home. I felt like I had come to a foreign land, and I did not know how to deal with the new people I met. My own relatives seemed strangers to me as I had built my own world back in Dubai. I was here to find myself, and this was not a reverse gear but an inward journey to seek my true self. This was a decision I had made, and it was my responsibility to ensure it worked for me. Bring me the much-needed peace and balance in my life.

> **Do not hold on to anything in life; nothing is permanent.**

Although the change was not easy, it taught me the most valuable lesson of life—*do not hold on to anything in life; nothing is permanent*. Six months later this lesson became all the more relevant when the entire world was forced to change their way of living due to the pandemic outbreak. By then I had made good progress, and it was not at all difficult for me to accept the unexpected change that was forced on all of us. In fact, it was the finest time for me to apply my knowledge and skills to progress in my journey of achieving my purpose.

Patience is a virtue they say, and indeed it has been one for me. We correlate balance in life to conditional things like job, family, success, and fame. But this is where I learned that you are all alone on this journey. The balance in your life does not come with fulfilling your conditions in life but by making peace with conditions around you. You find balance by making friends with yourself first, instead of the hundreds of people around you. You find balance by accepting what has happened to you and acknowledging that you are vulnerable and nothing is in your control. You find balance when you connect to the power of Almighty, which is the biggest source of strength in life. You find balance when you understand that we are too small to take things for granted.

The next few months were a roller-coaster ride for me. I had made a conscious decision not to be harsh on myself nor force myself to bounce back. I wanted to give myself time and never wanted to do things that seemed overwhelming, even if it meant I did not pursue what I most loved, public speaking. My mind and heart were not ready to handle the slightest of pressure, and I wanted to be kind to myself. I was on a journey of consciously understanding myself and the person with me, my mom. All my life I was complaining about how unfair my mom had been with me as she left me alone. I believe this was an opportunity to put an end to all of those qualms. I had realized that

> *What has happened to you so far is not in your control; what happens in your future is your responsibility.*

During the first six months of my time when I was emotionally vulnerable, my mom was my biggest strength. She stood by me and helped me settle so well that I got very close to her. Although we had our arguments during the first few months, it was all about to dilute in my journey of discovering myself.

Don't we all have to come back to our roots one day—dead or alive? This is where I faced an epiphany that eventually one has to come back to their mother's lap when they are lost. You may have traveled thousands of miles and built miles of dwellings that are sparingly used. But eventually, our heart travels back thousands of miles to where it began, in search of comfort and peace. Traveling back to your root does not always have to be going back to where you were born. An inward journey into yourself is also where your root to your existence prevails.

Who Do You Think You Are?
After a few days of my arrival in India, I was asked to go for a medical checkup by my insurance company, so I could get a new coverage for myself. My appointment was at 9:00 a.m., and I reached the hospital on time. I was guided to the casualty section where the checkup was scheduled to take place. After my initial blood test, I had to undergo an ECG test to check the condition of my prized possession. . . . MY HEART.

As I entered the casualty room, the nurse made me lie down to check my blood pressure. The results showed a magic number of 110/70 that has been static for many years now. I was glad that blood pressure was just a number—till the time it was in control and mine lived up to my expectation. It was now time for my ECG, and the nurse asked me to shift to the bed on the opposite side. As I was preparing to get comfortable, I noticed an elderly patient lying on the bed nearby. The only thing that separated him from me was the vacant bed in between us.

> Some situations can change your entire perspective of life—experience it. This is where growth is guaranteed.

While he was being thoroughly attended by the duty doctor, I overhead the conversation between the doctor and the patient's relative. I stressed my ears and tried to make sense of the conversation that was turning out to be alarming. My eyes opened wide like a stretched rubber band.

In utter disbelief, I immediately asked the nurse, "Is he dead?" to which she casually replied, "Yes, he is."

I smiled in nervousness and asked, "And you have put me next to a dead body?"

Unapologetically, she replied, "Don't worry, there is a bed in between you and him."

This seemed like an analogy to the fact that the only thing that separated the deceased and me at that moment was the ability to breathe. The words of the nurse were like a beam of light that struck my face with the stark realization of the reality of life. As my ECG began, some profound thoughts ran through my mind, making me think about what had just happened. My thoughts reverberated with the realization that "The only reason we are able to laugh, eat, hurt, complain, cry is because we have the capacity to breathe. The day this privilege is taken away from us then we are no different from this dead man next to me." So, what are we proud of? What makes us think that we ARE what we have achieved? This was my first realization of the stark reality of life. After returning home, I thanked God for this experience as it only made my inward journey easier.

Accept Unconditionally

When we moved to India, my kids insisted that we get a pet dog. Although I am a dog lover, I have never felt it right to have a dog in an apartment. As a child, I have personally grown up with pets around me and I am fully aware of the positive impact it can have in our life. But living in an apartment in

Dubai and having a pet at home was not on my agenda, and thus I did not give in to my kids' request.

The building management in India too did not allow pet dogs in the apartment and the only option was a cat. This was not my personal favorite, and I kept procrastinating the idea until one day my husband was dragged into this by my daughter. She managed to convince my husband, who gave in to her demand easily. I initially thought it was a joke until I saw a brown Persian kitten at home. I was not happy and told my kids that it would be their responsibility to take care of the kitten and I am not going to be involved. Finally, this kitten ended up being my responsibility since my kids had to go to school. Unwillingly, I forced myself to do the chores and was skeptical about how long I could sustain this routine. After a week I asked my kids to return the kitten to the pet shop as it was not working for me.

> *Have a pet at home when you are going through a rough patch. Their presence is simply therapeutic.*

My kids were not happy with the idea and instead named him "Loki," the main antagonist in the Marvel Cinematic and also the God of Mischief. For me, he seemed to be the antagonist in my life who was giving me a hard time. But slowly and steadily I noticed a significant change in the way things were shaping up around me. My children spoke less about Dubai and were totally involved with Loki and his mischief. They cleaned him, fed him, and also showed conscious responsibility toward Loki's well-being. Loki too started getting comfortable and loved playing with us and having fun. While I was witnessing all of this happening around me, I also felt a strange change in the way I felt about Loki. I could see myself treating him like a baby and ensuring that he was well fed and taken care of. I loved playing with him before going to bed and would call out his name as I woke up in the morning. In no time Loki has become a part of our family who brought a lot of joy and laughter at home. Today Loki is inseparable and we all love him to the bits.

As Loki became a part of our family, I also saw myself shedding the barriers that I had built in my mind about cats. I was surprised that accepting Loki wholeheartedly was the best thing that had happened to me. This was an epiphany to how beautiful life can get when we break our mental barriers and accept things as they are. Thinking about it, there are so many barriers that we have built that are stopping us from experiencing life. Most of the time it is not life that puts us in a certain situation, but it is we who are responsible for it. This has much to do with the expectations that we set for ourselves, which in reality are barriers that stop us from progressing. Loki taught me that making things better was in my own hands and no one else can do it for me. Similarly, your life is your responsibility, and no one will come to rescue you. When you face unexpected changes in your life, take a moment and think if there is anything that you could do to make things happen. Sometimes it is just a small shift in thinking that will show you a new ray of hope.

Pursuing Your Passion

While I had made a conscious decision to limit my social activity until I made good progress in my inward journey, over time I felt the need to keep myself busy. The best option was to pursue my public speaking activity. I took it slow and did not want to indulge in more than one meeting a fortnight. I must confess that I was not able to connect with the members in my new club, OR probably I was not ready to connect. All this while I was used to giving speeches which said, "Life begins at the end of your comfort zone." Now it was my time to apply this to my life—get outside my comfort zone.

> **Take ownership of your journey and set your own rules, if that helps you. Keep doing what helps you move forward.**

It was a new environment and a brand-new life that I was beginning. I had no expectation nor was I in a race to prove anything to anyone. But if there was one thing I did, it was to continue my journey of self-improvement, be it through trainings or through the conscious effort of self-development.

My focus was to experience everything that was going around me and accept it as it is. While my husband and I kept our communication channel open, he was my strongest support for my well-being. We were living in two different countries and were both walking our individual journey toward a common goal. We were rediscovering our individual selves as well as the love and respect we had for each other. There were times we felt we were getting on each other's nerves. Thank God! We were not in the same house. We would laugh at what life had put us through, and at the same time, both of us were excited to share our experiences. When one of us was down the other one picked up and sometimes both of us put each other down, yet the beauty was to pick up that phone and talk for hours together. It was a conscious time for both of us to redefine the meaning of our life. I had to take ownership of everything that was happening and stop blaming my parents, the circumstances, and everything else in the world.

This was the most grounded phase of my life, learning what mattered and what did not. Slowly but steadily I opened myself up to the new world and new set of people. Each and every person I met, I accepted wholeheartedly. My mission from here onward was to learn every little thing I came across. I got enough opportunities to grow and get closer to experiencing myself in totality. Silently, I started building my mental resilience. From a time when I had decided to go on incognito mode, to my decision to bounce back to normalcy, there is one more important lesson I learned—***Pursue your passion, no matter what happens.***

Pursuing your passion by doing what you love will result in deriving value to others and yourself.

When people go through a rough patch, the tendency is to withdraw from the outer world. Unexpected events may overwhelm you and force you to do so, but it is always advisable to keep your connections with family and friends active. In fact, this is the time when you have to build connections and expand your network. Of course, there could be a few people who may not be interested in associating with you. But consider them as experiences of life and move on. Life is beautiful only when you build associations and conversations. Without people, you cannot get any far. Try to understand people even at your toughest times because this is where the true meaning of life lies. This will also help you deal with the unexpected change in life in terms of rebuilding your life or interests and maneuvering your life in a direction you always wanted.

The Mother I Thought I Never Knew

Slowly but steadily I was transforming and building my resilience. After a few months I had built my network of friends; I continued doing what I loved and was also taking courses that would help me explore the options that I wanted to pursue. I realized that this phase was the best thing that has ever happened to me because it gave me amazing experiences that I could share in this book. An entirely new world of opportunities was standing in front of me, and I had to just find a way to embrace them. I had also made great progress in my spiritual journey, which helped me bring clarity and strengthen my thoughts.

While the entire world was reeling under the COVID-19 effect, we were also trying to adjust to the new situation. We were getting self-reliant in getting the house chores done and also sourcing essential items. It was a reality check in our lives. Suddenly the virus seemed to have thrown a massive challenge to the entire world. As insignificant human beings, all of us were just trying to swim in the rough waters of uncertainty.

Under the massive waves of change, we were learning lessons that we would have not learned otherwise. Suddenly the shift was toward "being human" and less of "proving human." Every day came with a new challenge that posed a thought-provoking question to all of us—what is eventually important in life?

The lockdown was a major shift in the way people started living their lives. But for me, nothing had changed because I had already embarked on the journey of solitude for almost a year now. What was going around me just reiterated that I was on the right track and the universe was conspiring to transform me. I realized the value of each and every thing I had in my life, and my empathy toward others improved drastically and this time in a more profound manner. It was now time to test my progress levels.

But like always the universe was waiting to throw another challenge at me, and this time it was bent on completing my circle of life.

We were two weeks into the lockdown and trying to adjust to the new way of living. One Sunday afternoon I was having my lunch and talking to a friend on the phone when I heard a big sound in the kitchen. I saw a steel tumbler being thrown from one end to the other. As I was trying to make sense of what happened, I left my food on the dining table and rushed to the kitchen. I saw my mother on the floor, fallen on her stomach and screaming in pain.

"Mummy, what happened. How did you fall?" I asked.

She was not in a position to answer me nor did she allow me to hold her hands to help her sit straight. My kids came running to help their grandma but to no avail. The more we tried to make her sit, the more she screamed. Finally, after 30 minutes we managed to make her sit upright and then on the chair. It was a Sunday afternoon, and a strict lockdown was implemented in our city. The next thing I had to do was call an ambulance, but instead I called my cousin Suraj, who has always been our biggest pillar of support.

"Give me five minutes, I will be right there," he said.

He came with permission from the cops to drive to the hospital, and finally, my cousin and I managed to rush my mother to the hospital emergency care. My mom was in pain, and there was nothing that could help her stop crying. She was taken to the X-ray room and after some time the results showed that she had a massive fracture on her left shoulder, which meant she had to be on heavy cast for the next three weeks. After the treatment, we returned home, and my mom had to rest completely for three weeks.

My life for the next three weeks was full of chores, taking care of mom, my children, and also attending to my writing and training work. I had all the reasons to complain and blame everyone around me. Instead, something amazing was happening to me. I found peace and happiness in feeding my mom and giving her a bath. I felt energetic in doing the house chores and above all considered all of this as a blessing.

It was not me but someone else inside me perhaps!

While my mom found solace in blaming her fate for the mishap, I found wisdom in saying, "Mom, thank God it is not the leg and hand together. We can still manage things, don't worry. Three weeks will fly in a jiffy."

My new avatar took me by surprise. I thought to myself, "If it was one year back, my response to the whole situation would be extremely negative." I would have brought the whole world down, complained, and been irritated. But this time, I found extreme peace and happiness in taking care of my mom. The deep void that was inside me filled with pride that I was finally doing what a good daughter must do. If I had not been present when my mom fell down, perhaps she would be lying on the floor for hours together. I had never felt this way before, but this time I was in charge of my emotion, and I could clearly feel that I was directing it toward the direction of growth, happiness, and peace.

> *There is no time right or wrong for unexpected change to take place. What makes it so is how you deal with it.*

I had finally passed the test that the universe had put me through. I was finally at peace with myself. When people sympathized with what had happened, I stepped up like a warrior and asked them to see the brighter side. I realized that my mom had aged, and she needed me with her. The best thing I had done was to take a break from life and dedicate that time to her. It was all worth it, and my journey was finally taking shape. Life had come a full circle for me, and nothing mattered more than some good time spent with my mother. All the qualms I had about her had finally disappeared. I had learned to understand her emotions and why she had kept me away from her. I could feel her pain and regret that she had for which she could never forgive herself. But through this unexpected twist in my journey, I found my *"mother I thought I never knew."*

My life had indeed had come a full circle, and now I knew the true purpose of this journey to my root. It was the universe's way of helping me reconcile with my past and my emotions that were left unattended. This was possible only when I began the journey of self-discovery on my own. It was when I decided to slow down and make time to understand the valuable things in life. Making myself emotionally intelligent by handling my own emotions, understanding my mother, and increasing my empathy quotient helped me achieve greater stride. It resulted in greater focus and enthusiasm and helped me to be excited about my own life. It helped me create this book as I was experiencing my life in parallel.

Unexpected changes that take place in life could seem disruptive and could potentially bring you down to your knees. One has to go through the experience and emotions that the situation demands. But what you do next and how you decide to manifest this change. The finest tool that helped me was already within me. I had is totally up to you to just create awareness to understand it better, and I did it all by using this gift called "Emotional Intelligence."

My dad is surely smiling up there looking at me and reading some books on emotional intelligence ☺

Keys to Managing Unexpected Change

1. The journey begins with accepting change—experience it to grow in abundance.
2. Do not hold on to anything in life; nothing is permanent.

3. Some situations can change your entire perspective of life—experience it. *This is where growth is guaranteed.*
4. Have a pet at home when you are going through a rough patch. *Their presence is simply therapeutic.*
5. Take ownership of your journey and set your own rules if that helps you. Keep doing what helps you move forward.
6. Pursuing your passion by doing what you love will result in deriving value to others and yourself.
7. There is no time right or wrong for unexpected change to take place. What makes it so is how you deal with it.

• • •

Pearls of Wisdom

1. Let your experience be your game changer.
2. Do not be in a rush to get back in control.
3. Pursue your passion.
4. Avoid others' perception to be your reality.
5. Speak positive language.
6. Pursue change proactively.
7. Choose faith over fear.

Conclusion

Change has been a part of human existence forever and it has always given us hope to do things differently. Change is welcoming when it is a part of your plan, but when it is not it creates unpleasant situations.

We call such unpleasant twists and turns in life as unexpected changes, especially when change happens when everything seems to be going great. If you look around you will find innumerable stories of people who have gone through these unexpected changes; some have given up, yet some have faced the heat and moved along.

We all face changes in life, but an unexpected change is like being attacked by your enemy when you are not prepared for the war. When this is the case, the only option you have is to surrender or fight back. How many of you have surrendered to the challenges? Is it because you could not handle the situation, or you did not want to handle it? Most of the time we tend to immerse ourselves in thinking what has gone wrong and what could have gone right. While this is what most people do, what we don't realize is that we are the reason for most of our worries because of the disconnect between the heart and mind, which often forces us to wander in the space of denial and resistance.

There are many reasons why life can be affected, and reasons such as divorce, job loss, financial issues, bankruptcy, health issues, or even a death of a loved one are some of the major ones. These unexpected changes could knock at your door any time, making life difficult, especially when a lot has been taken for granted with the success and comfort in life. But how many of you really speak about such events taking place in your life? Imagine if you are able to learn some valuable lessons from your own life, how powerful could your state of mind get? While we all take inspiration from the life of successful people, we seldom notice people who have bounced back after a fall from a high.

After writing this book I am reassured that every experience in life is valuable, and each experience is here to teach you profound insights as a guiding light. After achieving what I wanted to, I too was a bit bored of the monotonous routine of life. There was nothing much to look forward to as everything seemed settled. But what I realized is that it is at such a time the deeper aspects of life surface and make you introspect. Which means that whatever stage in life you are, you have to certainly take care of the person inside you. Emotions are the core of your existence, and even if you ignore them, they will find a way to resurface and distract you. Like in my case they had the potential to change the way I lived my life.

CONCLUSION

I was not aware that life could spiral down from such a high for reasons beyond the obvious. I had seen my dad lose out on business after achieving success. But I was still very young then and thought my dad was strong enough to handle it. But little did I know that "It is not the strongest of the species that survive, nor the most intelligent, but the most responsive to change" (Charles Darwin).

But how can one be responsive to change without someone guiding them? It may all seem easy to say, but when reality strikes, we all lose our mind, and how we react could be anything but rational. But you must have heard about the 21/90 rule, where it takes twenty-one days to create a habit, ninety days to create a lifestyle. Which means even handling unexpected changes comes with a conscious decision to be emotionally intelligent. Although I was not aware that my footsteps were in that direction, I could see that this direction was helping me balance my mind and heart as I realized that understanding yourself is the key to any external development.

This is what the book brings to light, human existence under adversity. No one is immune to change, but how you handle it sets the direction of your future. This book focuses on the journey and the learnings that I have had much later in life. Your life is the sum of your experience, and that has been the case in my life for sure. It is only when you cherish these experiences that you start valuing your life and what happens to you.

Another angle this book highlights is that facing an unexpected event is not the end of your journey but is the beginning to many new experiences. The different chapters in this book focus on topics that pave the path to building our future. We often focus a lot on material gains to validate our success but forget that what determines our success is our attitude, ability to make thoughtful decisions, self-awareness, empathy, managing stress, and ability to turn challenges into opportunities. This is what made a difference in my life—eventually realizing that life is much more than what you think it is.

Life as explained in this book reflects on the journey of a young me living away from my parents to becoming independent at a very young age. This book is about my journey and how I lived a life that was filled with the kind of thinking that defined who I am. All these traits helped me build my life and adopt an attitude that supported my husband and me to build a life that we wanted. But it was only when I crossed my prime age of 35, I realized that emotions also need to be addressed just the way you care for your family. You have to take care of the deeper self that is inside of you as it can potentially disrupt your life.

True to this that it did disrupt my life as the trauma that I had gone through losing my dad resurfaced. This clearly had not been addressed as I was busy building my life. Isn't it true in most cases? We are so busy in achieving our goals that we ignore ourselves to such an extent that life has to take a firm step to make us realize it.

With me it was only when I had attained a level of success that my life took a different direction. It had sort of spiraled down to a level that threw my life out of control. It was hard to put it together without external help or some drastic move from my end. Although I was not sure what was the best way forward, I just did what seemed right because this time I listened to myself.

Understanding my emotions and what was happening to me gave me the much-needed clarity to gain back my confidence and balance. In the world of psychology, I was being emotionally intelligent. It was only when I got introduced to this topic, I learned that the willingness to learn from your experience makes you emotionally intelligent. Unknowingly, I was being emotionally intelligent, thanks to my exposure to public speaking. I had learned to be comfortable talking about myself in my speeches, increasing interaction with people, and being comfortable with not being comfortable.

This is why each of the main chapters discusses the main topic in relation to emotional intelligence and its importance. All these years emotional intelligence was still not a hot topic of discussion. But in recent times with people talking about mental illness in open, the real worth of emotional intelligence has been highlighted. More and more people realize that emotional intelligence is the only way in which people can overcome their challenges because it all begins with "you."

Getting back your life in control is a result of how you handle your emotions during challenging times. Changing the world may be difficult, but changing yourself is much easier, and a change is a change when you change.

Today as I have completed this book, I have gained a lot of clarity in my thought and speech, making it easy for me to look ahead. It has also made me realize that life is not meant to be taken so seriously that one day you would break down. It is okay to be vulnerable and not have answers to all your questions. Life is a continuous process of gaining knowledge, but the bigger good you do is when you apply this knowledge for your own growth and be kind to yourself.

The change in direction in my life helped me align my thoughts and build a meaningful relationship not only with the world but even with myself. Spent good time with my children who are the biggest pillars of support. Learned that the man in my life, my husband, is nothing less than a warrior – a true gem.

Although I have hit my mid-forties, and for the world it may seem a bit late, for me my life has just begun. I just can't wait to embrace my exciting future that was built bit by bit with patience, mistakes, and learnings. If it wasn't for this experience of mine, my life would have never aligned with my purpose in life – LIVE IN THE NOW. After all, it is in these small moments that you make bigger moments of tomorrow.

The value this book can add to the readers can only be determined by the way my personal journey has manifested. The main three takeaways from this book would be

1. Accept that life is not going to remain the same forever.
2. Emotional mastery plays a key role in determining your future.
3. Your journey can be someone else's guide to survival — share it.

CONCLUSION

The book's mission is to reach out to all the female readers over mid-thirties who are facing unexpected change in their life. However, this could also serve as a guide to people of all ages as unexpected change does not see age and gender. The very fact that you are reading the end means that my mission is certainly accomplished.

Let me remind you that it is okay to feel the way you are doing, and do not judge yourself based on what you are going through now. Instead, invest the time and effort into focusing on your own inward journey and growth.

Your task on hand is to understand how you can make this journey better by getting into the depth of your own emotion and not wait for the unexpected change to happen.

"BACK IN CONTROL"

Is moving forward and creating an amazing life and not struggling to get your old life back.

References

http://www.agiftofinspiration.com.au/stories/attitude/starfish.shtml

https://mike-robbins.com/the-power-of-empathy/

https://daniels.du.edu/blog/emotional-intelligence-key-effective-leadership/

https://www.inc.com/justin-bariso/how-to-increase-your-emotional-intelligence.html

https://blog.iqmatrix.com/embrace-change

http://press.careerbuilder.com/2011-08-18-Seventy-One-Percent-of-Employers-Say-They-Value-Emotional-Intelligence-Over-IQ-According-to-CareerBuilder-Survey

https://scholar.harvard.edu/files/jenniferlerner/files/annual_review_manuscript_june_16_final.final_.pdf

www.ingramcontent.com/pod-product-compliance
Lightning Source LLC
Chambersburg PA
CBHW021439080526
44588CB00009B/591